INSTANT POT COOKBOOK #2020

500 EASY AND HEALTHY INSTANT POT RECIPES COOKBOOK FOR COMPLETE BEGINNERS AND ADVANCED USERS

ELIZABETH GREEN

ISBN: 978-1-950284-51-1

ISBN: 978-1-950284-51-1

DISCLAIMER

Please note, the information contained in this book, are for educational purposes only. Every attempt has been made to provide accurate, up to date and reliable complete information. By reading this document, the reader agrees that under no circumstances are we responsible for any losses, direct or indirect, which are incurred as a result of the use of the information contained in this document, including but not limited to errors, omissions or inaccuracies.

Table of Contents

INTRODUCTION

We are living in a world where you must multitask to make the best use of days and make every hour count for productivity. How does it feel to go to the bed while your food is cooking and wake up the next morning to find your food ready? Better still, would you like to go to work and come back in the evening and find your food cooked?

These may not be new to you. There has been a kitchen gadget that does that and much more. A gadget in the kitchen? Yes, you read that well! It categorizes more than a common utensil that you stack with other pots. We are here talking about the instant pot.

You may have acquired an instant pot. But are you using it to the best? Maybe your mom has one. Or is it your boss? It could also be that you're considering ordering yours. The electric cooking appliance was introduced to the market in 2012 as a 6-in-1 pot and improvements have been made in subsequent years.

As you continue to read this Book, you'll see how much benefit you can derive from it due to the comfort in cooking it offers to the users. You will also see how easy it has made it to put together various recipes into delicious meals.

This book has been purposely made for the benefit of a greater number of people who love to explore their culinary skills to various levels. It is not just about what the Instant Pot is and how it works. It also explores what you can do with it.

Call it a recipe book and you will be 100 percent correct. It is actually a cookbook. It contains scores of recipes in its 21 chapters. This book explores deeper beyond recipes for common food items like pastas, eggs, and maybe broths. It may interest you to know that the instant pot is also versatile for cooking recipes for specialized diets and tantalizing meals will be made.

For instance, are you a vegetarian or are looking to incorporate vegetarianism into the instant pot? This book has a lot of options for you. Also, a whole chapter has been devoted to taking care of the desires of those exploring gluten-free instant pot cooking. The paleo diet recipes have been carefully included. Even the strict keto diet has not been excluded in this book. It contains tested and well-researched recipes that are compatible with your vegetarian and keto goals.

There are protein-packed meals with various recipes for soups, desserts, and cakes made in the instant pot. There is something for almost everyone here as it contains perfect substitute for whatever you'll like to avoid or include.

It's my hope that you'll enjoy reading this book and be inspired to make the best use of this versatile cooking gadget. Please do enjoy your new Instant Pot cooking and your meal!

CHAPTER 1: ABOUT THE INSTANT POT

What is the Instant Pot? That may mean a little to you if you've been using an instant pot for some time. Well, an instant pot is a combination of electric cooking appliances. It is a pressure cooker, rice cooker, slow cooker, yogurt cooker, and many more in one appliance. It is a multifunctional cooker.

It is a versatile electric cooking utensil that you will love to have by you all the time as it fits your cooking needs no matter how your night or day is. After a frenetic day, for instance, you may need just a fast meal by throwing together a few items that should be ready within minutes. The instant pot can do just that for you.

At some other times, you may plan to get home late and want to avoid cooking late in the night. In such cases, you will find a slow cooker useful to get your dinner ready for you to just munch with pleasure upon arrival at home. It is the appliance that cooks your food with the pace you set. That means you can depend on it to adjust to the peculiarity of any day.

Differences Between the Instant Pot and Conventional Pressure Cookers

Please do not confuse a pressure cooker with the instant pot. Yes, they have a number of functional similarities. But there are remarkable differences. While the pressure cooker is ordinary kitchenware, the Instant Pot makes use of programmable electronic control. Conventional pressure cookers do not have this feature. That is why the instant pot is being described as the electronic form of the pressure cooker. The electronic programming enables it to cook with more consistency.

Another difference is the integrated heating unit that is an integral feature of the instant pot. This makes it safer and energy-efficient. As for the conventional pressure cooker, the source of heat is external. It is either heated by a gas stove or connected to an electrical outlet to generate heat.

Differences Between the Instant Pot and Slow Cooker

While the Instant Pot can cook slowly, it is not essentially a slow cooker as it can cook at very high temperature. On the other hand, a slow cooker, cooks only at low temperature. Foods cooked in the Instant Pot get ready much earlier than the ones cooked in the slow cooker; it is 70% faster.

That means on days you are racing against time, you can count on the instant pot to speed up your cooking. You may, for instance, come home late and do your prepping in a few minutes and toss everything into the instant pot while you have your shower. In about 30 minutes the whole thing is ready.

Features of the Instant Pot

The following are the features of the instant pot:

1. **High safety standard:** It is safe to use with 10 safety mechanisms and technologies built with it. It also has the UL certification.
2. **Versatility:** It is useful for braising, fermenting, making yogurt, and keeping warm in addition to pressure cooking, sautéing/ browning, simmering, steaming, and stewing.
3. **Convenient:** It is being controlled by a microprocessor, it is convenient for cooking. You just need to press any of the function keys and relax until your meal is cooked. It is the in-built microprocessor that will do the job of controlling the time, cooking temperature and cooking pressure.
4. **Flexibility:** It has dual pressure setting. It can be either fast or flexible in cooking. You can set it to high pressure to gain 70% of the cooking time or set it at low pressure to avoid overcooking a delicate food.
5. **Manual cooking time selection:** You can select the manual cooking of up to 240 minutes.
6. **Auto keep-warm:** Even after cooking, the auto keep-warm function starts automatically and runs for 10 hours.
7. **Easy to clean:** It is made with stainless steel that is dishwasher safe. So you can throw the parts into your dishwasher and watch it washed clean.
8. **Bluetooth compatibility:** The Instant Pot smart is Bluetooth-friendly. It can be wirelessly connected to your smartphones.
9. **It is clean and pleasant.**
10. **It has long hours of delayed cooking.**

CHAPTER 2: THE BENEFITS OF THE INSTANT POT

You may be no stranger to the Instant Pot. You are probably familiar with the speed with which it cooks. If you knew it quite well, you will realize that it has some other benefits. In case you did not know, the Instant Pot has the following benefits.

1. It Saves Time and Energy

The instant pot has energy efficiency due to the following two major factors, namely:

Its cooking chamber, that is the inner pot, is fully insulated. That is why the cooker does not have to consume much energy before heating up. The second is that you do not have to add much liquid before your meal in the Instant Pot is cooked, it actually boils faster.

Also, when compared to other cooking methods like baking, boiling, roasting, steaming and stovetop, the Instant Pot cooking requires less cook time. So it saves time by up to 70 percent and reduces the energy usage by the same margin. It reaches temperatures above boiling translating to fast cooking.

2. It Requires Less Water

When steaming in an Instant Pot, up to 75% less water is needed compared to other cooking methods. Again, it is also great for energy efficiency because it will require less energy as you will need to heat or boil less water.

3. It Has Intelligent Programming

It has one-touch programs that have been carefully tested and refined based on a series of experiments. Each of the presets has been designed for consistency in cooking results. It is this intelligent programming that ensures cooking is consistent irrespective of the volume and quantities. For instance, it takes the same amount of time to cook one egg and one dozen eggs. You can still have more fine-tuning for most programs. And the Instant Pot can save and remember your setting such as your preference for a shorter or longer.

4. It Is Fully Insulated

The Instant Pot cooker base is completely insulated. It has two layers of air pockets situated between the stainless steel exterior and the inner pot. Thus, while the internal temperature exceeds boiling points, the base of the cooker is safe to touch even when the cooking process is long.

This again saves energy as it only heats the inner pot to keep the pressure level. The intelligent programming prevents it from constantly exerting energy in maintaining heat. It engages the element in just 60% of the time during a cook cycle. Thus, it won't heat your home during summertime when you're already struggling with the ferocious heat outside. That means that you will consume less energy on air conditioning.

5. It Retains Vitamins and Nutrients

When you boil or even steam your food in the normal fashion, the water-soluble vitamins will leach out of it. This process reduces the nutritional value of your food. But an instant pot cooks deeply, evenly, and quickly thus allowing your food to retain as much as 90 percent of the water-soluble vitamin contents. This preservation of nutrition may also be due to the limit of its temperatures which maxes somewhere around 250°F (121°C). So it makes your meals healthier. Due to the advanced tech of its embedded microprocessor, you have the total control of your cooking cycles to prepare delicious meals.

6. It Preserves Food's Appearance and Taste

You notice that when you cook in a container that exposes its content, even the one with a lid, your food is exposed to oxygen and heat. This alters the color of the food and reduces its flavor. But the airtight Instant Pot environment saturates your foods with steam which allows the retention and preservation of colors, phytochemicals, and flavors as all are trapped inside their respective ingredients.

7. It Eliminates Harmful Microorganisms

The Instant Pot allows your water to boil beyond 212°F (100°C), thereby guaranteeing the destruction of harmful bacteria in your food. Thus, it is good water treatment. That is why it is advisable to use it as a sort of sterilization tool for baby bottles or jars.

8. It Is Convenient

Thanks to Instant Pot's preset Smart Programs features, it is convenient for the following:

- Beans and chili
- Congee/Porridge
- Keep warm
- Meat and stew
- Multigrain
- Rice
- Sauté/Browning
- Slow Cook

- Soup
- Steaming
- Yogurt of all sorts and makings

9. Automatic Cooking

It provides a fully automated process of cooking by timing each step of the task. The Instant Pot cooker can switch automatically from preheating to the cook cycle. Once the cooking is complete, it switches to "Keep Warm." This automatic cooking is greatly beneficial because you do not need to keep watching the cooking timer or monitoring the temperature levels. You do not have to be frequenting your kitchen to make your meal come out fine. You do not have to worry about overcooking. The Instant Pot comes with sensors for temperature and the pressure levels and it has other self-regulating features.

Though you have a 7-in-1 appliance, it is not so complicated to use. The automated cooking is activated with a few buttons to use with an understanding of a few basic tips.

10. Planning Meals With Delayed Cooking Made Easy

The Instant Pot can delay your cooking for up to 24 hours while your ingredient will not lose any part of its taste or spoil. That means you can set it to start cooking much later; for as long as a day. This is a great asset for a perfect meal planning. It is also cool for foods that are not in their best when frozen or refrigerated—beans, potatoes, rice and so on.

It also has short-term delay such that it can start your cooking in less than 2 hours which is also great for meal prepping. For instance, by reprogramming your main course, you have freed a lot of time to spend in preparing appetizers, desserts, and sides. Again, it affords you the opportunity to produce a tasty and healthy meal while not physically present in the kitchen.

11. It Aids Tenderness and Taste of Meats

When it comes to cooking those tougher cuts of meat, the Instant Pot cooking does it better than any other. It breaks down tough proteins and intramuscular fats quickly so that the meat can easily fall off the bone and eating is no struggle. Beans and legumes that can take all the time to get cooked can also be firmly cooked in reduced space of time.

12. It Cooks in a Clean and Pleasant Way

You do not have any struggle with a rattling steam-spewing monsters pot. The Instant Pot cooking is sleek and almost inaudible during cooking. It locks in aromas and flavors as observed, so your visitors hardly have an idea of when and what you are cooking. And it keeps your kitchen clean firstly, by reducing the number of appliances, and secondly by not spilling or spewing smokes.

13. No Need to Defrost In Microwave

Frozen foods cooked in the Instant Pot do not need defrosting. You, therefore do not need microwaving or wait for some time for your meat to defrost before you start cooking. Just toss them straight into the Instant Pot and there you go! In just a moment, you have finished a delicious meal.

CHAPTER 3: GRAINS RECIPES

The Instant Pot can be a fantastic tool for cooking for any recipe you can think of. Even grains are happy to feed you after passing through the pot. While many grains take a while to cook, some cook more quickly and more easily. Whichever way, the Instant Pot can provide you a lot of options to enjoy grains.

You might be surprised by the number of grain options that you can choose from. This chapter will give you some recipes ideas of various grains you can choose from and how you can easily cook them in your Instant Pot.

Oatmeal

Oatmeal doesn't really need an introduction because it is a staple throughout the world. So nutritious and versatile, oats are a rich source of fiber and are easy to cook. Oatmeal can be a fabulous breakfast for you if you make a quick meal or steel cut in the Instant Pot.

Ingredients

- 1 ¼ cups of water for creamier and thick bowl or 1 ½ cups of water for a moister bowl
- Your favorite nuts (as much as desired)
- Nut butter (as desired)
- Your favorite fruits (as much as desired)
- ½ cup of steel cut oat

Instructions

1. At high pressure, cook the oats for 10 minutes.
2. Allow the pressure to gradually release naturally for about 12 more minutes.
3. Top with all your favorite ingredients and super foods.

Yield: 2 cups of steel cut oat.

Barley: Hulled Barley

Barley is not just about beer. You can make a meal that is rich in plant source of protein from it. Try this healthy and lovely grain in the Instant Pot as described below and make a great meal.

Ingredients

- 1 cup of hulled barley
- 2 ½ cups of water or stock
- 1 tsp. of salt
- Bay leaf (optional)
- Olive oil or butter (to taste)

Instructions

1. Rinse the hulled barley in a mesh sieve and drain.
2. Pour the well-drained barley into the inner insert of the Instant Pot.
3. Add water or stock, salt and bay leaf (if using).
4. Close the lid and ensure you have the valve set to "sealing."
5. Set your Instant Pot to 23 minutes on multigrain function.
6. Once cooked, let the pressure release naturally, allowing at least 15 minutes. Then turn the valve to venting carefully and let the pin drop. Open the lid.
7. Use a fork or wooden spoon to fluff the barley. Never mind the presence of water. Leave it or drain it.
8. Then stir in olive oil.

Yield: 3 cups.

Millet (Porridge)

Millet is the alternative to many other whole grains and can be a part of any dish on breakfast. Its taste and texture make it a good rival for quinoa or oatmeal. Try it in your Instant Pot as explained below.

Ingredients

- 1 cup of millet
- 3 tbsp. of brown sugar (or as desired)
- 1 ½ tsp. of cinnamon
- 1 ½ tbsp. of unsalted butter
- 6 tbsp. of raisins
- 3 cups of milk
- Frozen berries for serving (optional)
- Milk or cream for serving (optional)

Instructions

1. Pour one cup of water to the Instant Pot with a trivet inside.
2. Combine all the ingredients in a glass dish that fits into the Instant Pot. Cover with foil and place on the trivet.
3. Carefully close the lid and turn the valve to "sealing."
4. Depending on the model of your Instant Pot, press Pressure Cooker or Manual button and select 12 minutes using the arrows. It will produce pressure after about 5 minutes.
5. Once the cooking is done after the 12 minutes, wait for 10 minutes for natural pressure release and then do a quick release which takes just a few seconds.
6. Carefully remove the bowl containing the millet porridge from the Instant Pot.
7. Open the foil and mix very well to ensure that the milk is fully absorbed. If not, cover with foil and wait for 3 to 5 minutes more and serve hot. You may add the optional berries and a few splashes of cream or milk.

Yield: 4 servings.

Dried Corn or Popcorn

It's amazing to many and unimaginable to others that you could make your popcorn in your Instant Pot. The fact is that you could enjoy this low-calorie as a nighttime snack if you use sauté technique in your Instant Pot.

Ingredients

- 2 tbsp. of organic refined coconut oil
- 1 tbsp. of butter unsalted
- ½ cup of corn kernels
- Ground pepper, salt, or other seasonings of your choice (all optional)

Instructions

1. Turn the Instant Pot to Sauté. Set the temperature to More and allow the display to turn to Hot
2. Add the butter and coconut oil and allow to melt, then combine well.
3. Add corn kernels.
4. Sauté for a minute to allow the corn kernels to be well coated with oil and butter.
5. Close the pot with a well-fitted glass lid.
6. Allow the popping to start and continue for 5 about minutes when it should have slowed down.
7. Turn off your Instant pot or click on the "Cancel" button.
8. Never mind the moisture that will build under the glass lid and the slight dripping. Just carefully wipe off using your kitchen towel.
9. With oven mitt worn on your hand, open the Instant Pot lid and stir well the popcorn.
10. You can now season with any of your chosen optional seasonings and enjoy your crispy and best tasting snack.

Yield: 2 servings.

Bulgur Wheat Pilaf

Bulgur is a meal you can try out if you are looking for another way to serve your whole wheat. It is a humble, fiber-rich grain that you can explore in several ways. You love it the more if you make a pilaf of it using your Instant Pot.

Ingredients

- 1 tbsp. of olive oil
- 1 tbsp. of butter
- 3 tbsp. of onion (finely chopped)
- 2 tbsp. of celery (finely chopped)
- 1 medium cup of bulgur wheat (uncooked)
- 2 cups of chicken broth
- ½ tsp. of table salt
- ½ tsp. of Italian seasoning
- Lime wedges (optional garnish)
- Chopped cashews (optional garnish)
- Fresh chives (optional garnish)

Instructions

1. Open the lid of the Instant Pot (preferably 6-quart) and add the butter and olive oil to the inner pot.
2. Press Sauté and cook until the butter melts.
3. Add celery and onion. Cook and stir constantly every 2 minutes.
4. Add bulgur and stir to coat with oil.
5. Stir in chicken broth, Italian seasoning, and salt.
6. Turn off the cooker, then close and lock the lid of your Instant Pot. Release the handle to "Sealing" position.
7. Select the "Rice" function and cook for 12 minutes at Low Pressure.
8. After the 12 minutes, remove the lid by using "Quick Pressure Release." Fluff your pilaf with a fork and add the desired garnish.

Yield: 4 - 6 servings.

Quinoa Porridge

Though a seed, quinoa is a nutty-tasting food which comes in both red and white varieties. But it is a little more like a grain when you consider how it cooks. It is a source of plant protein containing all essential amino acids. All these can be preserved if you cook it in the Instant Pot.

Ingredients
- 1 ½ cup of quinoa (to be rinsed)
- 1 ½ cup of water (you can use stock)
- 1 teaspoon of kosher salt (omit or reduce if using stock)

Instructions
1. Rinse well the quinoa but do not soak.
2. Combine with water and salt (or stock without salt) into the inner pan of the Instant Pot.
3. Tightly seal the Instant Pot by ensuring that the vent knob is firmly on Seal.
4. Set the pressure to "High" and cook for 1 minute.
5. Allow the pressure to release naturally (it takes about five minutes) and turn the valve to release the rest of the steam.
6. Fluff with a fork or spoon and serve as desired.

Yield: 6 servings.

Cherry Amaranth Porridge

Amaranth is another grain that is rich in plant protein and fiber. It is gluten-free and contains a lot of minerals including copper, magnesium, zinc, and selenium. The calcium contents are also great especially if try this Cherry Amaranth Porridge is cooked in the Instant Pot pressure cooker.

Ingredients

- 1 cup of amaranth
- 1 cup of soy milk (plain)
- 1 cup of water
- 2 tsp. of ground cinnamon
- ½ tsp. of ground cardamom
- pinch of sea salt
- 1 to 2 cups of frozen dark cherries
- ½ cup of pecan pieces (unsalted)
- Maple syrup (as an optional topping)

Instructions

1. Add amaranth, cardamom, cinnamon, cherries, soy milk, sea salt, and water in Instant Pot.
2. Set to "Sealing" after putting the lid on.
3. Set your Instant Pot high pressure
4. Press the porridge button.
5. When it beeps, reduce the pressure with a quick release to release the steam safely.
6. Simmer and let steam off to reduce the residual water.
7. Serve topped with maple syrup (if used) and pecans.

Yield: 4 servings.

Buckwheat Porridge

Buckwheat is another nice gluten-free grain that used in sweet dishes such as porridge and savory dishes also. Its popularity may be due to its health benefits and being a mild and nutty flavor. Its porridge will make a granola binding agent if you allow your Instant Pot to do justice to it

Ingredients
- 1 cup raw buckwheat (Groats)
- 1 banana (to be sliced)
- 3 cups of rice milk
- ¼ cup of raisins
- 1 tsp. cinnamon (ground)
- ½ tsp. of vanilla
- chopped nuts (optional)

Instructions
1. Rinse well buckwheat and combine with all ingredients in the Instant Pot
2. Close the lid and set the Instant Pot on manual high pressure for 3-6 minutes cooking time.
3. When timer beeps, turn off the pot and do a quick release carefully. Then wait for about 20 minutes for the natural release of steam.
4. After the pressure is released, open the lid carefully and stir porridge with a long spoon.
5. If desired, add more rice milk while serving for preferred consistency. You may also add your favorite milk or any non-dairy milk.
6. Sprinkle with chopped nuts, if desired.

Yield: 4 servings.

Taco Pasta

The Instant Pot can be a great way of cooking anything pasta. Think of what your spaghetti, macaroni, penne, bow-ties, and others will become of you try them out. Your cooking experience will be quite rewarding. Try out the Taco Pasta with these very simple recipes and instructions.

Ingredients
- 1 lb. of ground beef (lean)
- 1 oz. of taco seasoning
- 2 cups of water
- 8 oz. of tomato sauce
- 2 tbs. of butter or oil
- 2 cups of beef broth
- 8 oz. of small pasta (medium shells)
- 1 ½ C cheese (shredded, can be cheddar or Mexican blend)

Instructions
1. Read the instruction for the particular pasta you are using and halve it when using the Instant Pot.
2. Set the Instant Pot to sauté and add the ground beef. Keep breaking as it cooks.
3. Stir in your taco seasoning once the ground beef is browned and add beef broth, tomato sauce, and then pasta.
4. Cover and seal the lid and adjust the setting to manual and time to 5 minutes.
5. Once Instant Pot beeps after five minutes, quick release.
6. Turn off Instant Pot and carefully remove cover and stir.
7. Add cheese as a topping and cover again but without sealing.
8. Wait 1 or 2 minutes for the cheese to melt and serve with other toppings of choice.

Yield: 4 servings.

Polenta

Polenta is a humble way of making out of dried cornmeal a sumptuous dish. It is a yum for those you love. And it is also fine if you are thinking about slicing it and frying it later. Check out this Instant Pot recipe for such cooking of polenta.

Ingredients
- 5 cups water (you can use low-sodium chicken broth instead)
- 1 cup coarse cornmeal
- 1 tsp. salt
- 2 tbsp. of butter (optional, you can use coconut or ghee oil, or any fat of your choice).
- ½ cup of grated parmesan cheese (optional)

Instructions
1. Combine water or chicken broth with your butter, fat, or oil (if using) and add salt, all in the insert pot of an Instant Pot.
2. Sauté until it starts to simmer and then stir in the polenta and slowly whisk to combine.
3. After locking the lid in place, select manual button or valve and cook on High Pressure, setting it to 7 minutes.
4. Once the cooking completes, let the pot release pressure naturally which takes about 10 minutes.
5. Then release any remaining pressure by turning the sealing valve.
6. Gently lift the Instant Pot a few inches away from the counter by one of the handles and set it back to the counter. Repeat for a few times to remove any possible steam bubbles during the cooking.
7. Remove lid and stir polenta well until smooth.
8. Add butter and cheese, if using them and serve.

Yield: 6 servings.

Vegetable Couscous

Couscous is a traditional dish derived from crushed durum wheat and is a popular Middle Eastern cuisine. It has been prepared in a lot of ways and each method makes a delicious and nutritious meal. Here you find the Instant Pot recipes for a method of Vegetable Couscous.

Ingredients
- 1 tbsp. of butter or olive oil
- 2 bay leaves
- ½ large onion (chopped)
- 1 red bell pepper (large, chopped)
- 1 cup carrot (grated)
- 1 ¼ cup Isreali Couscous
- 1 ½ cup of water
- 1 tsp. of salt (or to taste)
- ½ tsp. of Garam masala
- 1 tbsp. of lemon juice
- Cilantro to garnish

Instructions
1. Start the instant pot and heat in sauté mode.
2. Add butter or olive oil to it.
3. Add the onions and bay leaves and sauté for 2 minutes.
4. Add the carrots and bell peppers and sauté again for one minute.
5. Add the couscous to "toast" it. Add Garam masala, salt, and water. Stir well to combine.
6. Adjust the setting of the pressure cooker to Manual for 2 minutes.
7. When it beeps, do natural pressure release for 10 minutes so as to release the pressure manually.
8. Fluff the couscous, then add the lemon juice when it is fully cooked. Serve hot, garnishing with cilantro.

Yield: 3 servings.

You may want to make more or less than the servings of different Instant Pot grain meal described here. That's no big deal, it is just a matter of just scaling up or down the quantities of the recipes respectively.

CHAPTER 4: RICE RECIPES

You remember that the Instant Pot can also function as a rice cooker. Now, imagine how tasty it will be to cook your rice in this pot! Interestingly, there's almost no limit to how you can cook rice. Consider treating your visitors, family, or even your stomach to rice burrito, basmati rice, and even rice pudding. This chapter highlights recipes for these and others so that your rice can come in a new fashion courtesy your Instant Pot.

Thai Pineapple Fried Rice

Ingredients

- 1 tbsp. corn oil
- 3 tbsp. cashews
- 1 ¼ cups water
- ¼ cup onion (finely chopped)
- ¼ cup scallions (finely chopped, white parts only)
- 2 green Thai chili (finely chopped)
- 1 cup of canned pineapple chunks
- ½ tsp. curry powder
- ¼ tsp. ground turmeric
- 4 tbsp. fresh basil leaves (roughly chopped and divided)
- 2 tsp. soy sauce
- 1 cup steamed of short-grain white rice (preferably a day old)
- 1 tsp. kosher salt

Instructions

1. Pour the vegetables and pineapple into the pot and select sauté.
2. Add the oil and once hot, add in the cashews and stir for 1 minute.
3. Add the chili, onion, and scallions. Sauté for 3 to 4 minutes until the onion is translucent.
4. Combine the pineapple, basil leaves, curry powder, soy sauce, turmeric, and salt with the rice and water and mix thoroughly.
5. Tightly close the lid by setting the valve to "Seal" and select Pressure Cook (you can also use Manual). Set the pressure to "High" and the time to 3 minutes.
6. After cooking, wait 3 minutes for natural pressure release. Then, do then quick release to let out any remaining pressure.
7. Unlock and remove the lid, wait 15 minutes. Then fluff with a fork and serve.

Yield: 4 servings.

Shredded Chicken and Rice Burrito Bowl

You can make your rice into a burrito, especially brown rice, in place of a tortilla. In this recipe, avocado replaces the cheese. Try this in your Instant Pot and see how rice can soak up your flavorful and nourishing broth.

Ingredients

- 3 cups brown rice
- 2 tbsp. extra-virgin olive oil
- 1 tsp. ground cumin
- 2 lbs. boneless, skinless chicken breasts
- ¼ tsp. cayenne pepper (or taco seasoning)
- 1 medium red or white onion (chopped)
- 4 oz. green chili (chopped or diced)
- 1 ½ cups of low-sodium chicken broth
- 15 oz. pinto beans (drained and rinsed)
- 2 medium avocados for garnish (pitted and sliced)
- fresh (chopped) cilantro for garnish
- Jalapeño (sliced) for garnish
- Prepped salsa for garnish (optional)

Instructions

1. Rinse and cook the brown rice for 5 minutes and set aside.
2. Pour the olive oil into the pot and select Sauté and add the olive oil to the inner pot to heat the oil and thereafter add place the chicken breasts in the pot. Allow each of the sides 2 minutes to brown.
3. Select "Cancel" so that you can add the cayenne pepper, cumin, green chili, onion, and broth.
4. Set the release knot in "Seal" to lock the lid and select "Pressure Cook or Manual." Cook on High pressure set time to 15 minutes.
5. When the pot beeps, release pressure naturally for 10 minutes and quick release any remaining pressure, then unlock and remove the lid.
6. Transfer each chicken broth to cutting board and shred with two forks. Return the shredded chicken to the pot and add pinto beans. Stir in the ingredients to combine.
7. Serve immediately in six bowls, sprinkling with the chicken mixture. Add all garnishes used to each bowl together with salsa.

Yield: 6 servings.

White Basmati Rice

The Instant Pot will give your basmati rice a facelift because you will end up with fluffier more nutritious rice that is easy to cook. While your nose may not hint you of what to expect, your palate will thank you if you handle it according to the instructions below.

Ingredients

- 2 cups white basmati rice (must be rinsed)
- 3 cups of water

Instructions

1. Combine rice and water in the inner pot.
2. Set the release knot in "Seal" to lock the lid into place and select "Pressure Cook or Manual." Cook on "High" pressure set time to 8 minutes.
3. When the pot beeps, quick release the pressure. Then unlock and remove the lid.
4. Serve the rice immediately.
5. It can be refrigerated for 5 days or up to 2 months if placed in an airtight container.

Yield: 2 - 4 servings.

Chai Spiced Rice Pudding With Roasted Grapes

Ingredients (for Rice Pudding)

- 1 cup medium-grain rice
- 1½ cups unsweetened plain almond milk (or other nondairy milk like soy or oat milk)
- 1 cup canned full-fat coconut milk (well-stirred)
- 2 tbsp. sugarless almond butter
- 1 tsp. pure vanilla extract
- 2 tsp. cinnamon (ground)
- ½ tsp. ground cardamom
- ½ tsp. freshly grated or ground nutmeg
- 1 tsp. ground ginger
- 1/8 tsp. ground cloves
- 1 tbsp. pure maple syrup (or coconut sugar)
- 4 soft Medjool dates (pitted, roughly torn into pieces)
- 1 cup water
- 1/8 tsp. kosher salt

Ingredients (for Roasted Grapes)
- 1 bunch of seedless grapes
- Olive oil
- Fresh thyme
- Kosher salt or sea salt

Instructions

1. Preheat the oven to 450°F (230°C) to roast the grape
2. Add all ingredients to the rice and water in the Instant Pot and stir to combine.
3. Tightly cover the lid and set the Pressure Release to Sealing. Cook at high pressure and select the Pressure Cook or Manual setting; set to cook for 10 minutes.
4. Meanwhile, spread the grapes out on a baking sheet and drizzle with oil, sprinkle with salt and thyme leaves and gently toss with hands. Bake for about 8 minutes or until the grapes begin to burst.
5. Once the Instant Pot timer beeps, allow natural pressure release for 5 minutes. Switch the Pressure Release knob to "Venting" to complete the release.
6. Open the lid and stir the pudding thoroughly. All extra liquid that has possibly built up will incorporate into the rice and thicken up. Then serve with the roasted grapes.

Yields: 4 servings.

Savory Korean Beef and Rice

This is irresistible. Check out how to make it below savory Korean rice and beef. You'll be glad you tried it.

Ingredients (for Rice Mixture)
- 1 ½ cups of long-grain white rice (rinsed)
- 1 ½ of cups water
- 2 tbsp. butter

Ingredients (for Beef Mixture)
- 1 ½ lbs. lean beef (93%, ground)
- 6 cloves garlic (minced)
- ½ cup soy sauce
- ½ cup water
- ¼ cup brown sugar
- 1 tbsp. ginger root (grated)
- 1 tbsp. toasted sesame oil
- ½ tsp. white pepper
- ¼ tsp. cayenne (or to taste)

Ingredients (for Garnish)
- Sliced green onions
- Sesame seeds

Instructions
1. Add all rice mixture ingredients in an Instant Pot-compatible casserole and set aside.
2. Add ground beef to the inner insert of the Instant Pot and sauté until it browns and no pink remains and keep breaking.
3. Add beef mixture ingredients and stir well.
4. Insert a steam rack and lower the casserole.
5. Select "Cancel" to turn off the pot and secure the lid.
6. Then select "Manual" or "Pressure Cook" function and program the Instant Pot for 8 minutes.
7. Once it beeps, allow natural pressure release for 10 minutes. Then quick-release the rest of the pressure.
8. Take the casserole out carefully and fluff rice with a fork.
9. Stir in the beef mixture. Serve with the garnishes.

Yield: 2 Servings.

Buttery Rice Pilaf With Turkey Meatballs

Ingredients

- 2 ½ cups turkey broth
- 1 cup raw white basmati rice
- ½ cup chopped frozen onion (or 1 small yellow or white onion; peeled and chopped)
- 2 tsp. of stemmed and minced fresh sage leaves (or 1 tsp. of dried sage)
- 1 tsp. stemmed fresh thyme leaves (or 1/2 tsp. of dried thyme)
- 1 ½ lbs. frozen mini (or bite-sized) turkey meatballs
- 2 tbsp. butter
- ½ tsp. table salt

Instructions

1. Combine the broth, onion, sage, thyme, and salt with rice in the Instant Pot. Set to "Sauté", pressure cook and stir occasionally until many wisps of steam rise from the liquid. Then add the frozen meatballs and stir. Add the butter after switching off the "Sauté" function.
2. Lock the lid tightly and pressure cook on "Max Pressure" for 10 minutes (or select Poultry and set for "High Pressure" for 12 minutes). Keep "Warm" setting switched off.
3. Quick-release pressure and wait for 10 minutes for pressure to be completely released.
4. Open the cooker and stir well, then serve.

Yield: 4 servings.

Russian Garlicky Beef and Rice

Ingredients

- 2 ½ cups brown rice (rinsed)
- ¼ cup olive oil
- 4 tbsp. butter
- 3 cups hot water
- 1 large onion (finely diced)
- 1 ½ cups carrots (shredded)
- 1 lbs. beef stew (cut into 3/4-inch pieces)
- 2 bay leaves
- 2 heads of garlic cloves (unpeeled)
- ½ tsp. black pepper
- ½ tsp. coriander
- ½ tsp. each cumin
- ½ tsp. paprika
- 1 tbsp. kosher salt
- ½ cup Italian parsley (optional, chopped)

Instructions

1. Pour oil to the Instant Pot and select the "Sauté" function and set to "High" or "More".
2. Add meat when oil is hot and wait for 5 minutes to brown. Then add butter and onion and keep sautéing for 3 - 4 minutes.
3. Combine all seasonings and with carrots and cook for 5 minutes while scraping the browns from the pot bottom using a wooden spoon.
4. Add bay leaves and spread rinsed rice evenly over the vegetables (don't stir).
5. Add in garlic heads side down to the rice and have all halfway submerged.
6. Pour the hot water directly over the garlic to soften.
7. Turn the pot off (select "Cancel") and secure the lid, tightly closing the vent.
8. On the pot select the "Manual or Pressure Cook" program to 30 minutes.
9. When it beeps, allow the pressure to naturally release for 10 minutes and quick-release the remaining pressure.
10. Remove the garlic and bay leaves. Set aside garlic and discard the leaves and stir rice mixture to combine.
11. Add parsley (if using) and stir to combine. Then, serve warm.

Yields: 6 servings.

Wild Mushroom Risotto

Ingredients

- 3 tbsp. olive oil (divided)
- 3 tbsp. butter (divided)
- 8 oz. crimini (or baby bella mushrooms, sliced)
- 8 oz. wild mushroom (like shitake, oyster, sliced or any other)
- 2 tbsp. soy sauce
- 2 shallots (finely diced)
- 1 ½ cups Arborio rice
- 1 tsp. celery seed
- ½ cup white wine
- 3 cups chicken broth (warmed) or vegetable
- 2/3 cup parmesan (grated)
- ¼ cup chopped Italian parsley (optional)
- Salt and pepper to taste

Instructions

1. Add 2 tablespoons of olive oil and 2 tablespoons of butter to the Instant Pot, select "Sauté" function and set "More or High."
2. Add mushrooms when both get hot and cook for 7 minutes, stirring occasionally. Then, drain off excess liquid.
3. Add soy sauce, stir and cook for 7 minutes also.
4. Add the remaining oil and butter and stir to melt.
5. Add shallots, celery seed, and rice and cook 3 minutes, stirring.
6. Add wine and scrape the brown bits from the pot bottom using a wooden spoon.
7. Add broth and stir. Turn the pot off (select "Cancel") and secure the lid, tightly closing the vent.
8. On the pot select the "Manual or PRESSURE COOK" program to 6 minutes.
9. When the time is up, quick-release the remaining pressure.
10. Stir risotto for about 2 minutes or until the desired consistency. Return to "Sauté" when needed.
11. Stir in parmesan cheese allow it melt and add seasonings as required.
12. Garnish with Italian parsley (if using) and serve immediately.

Yield: 3 servings.

Cilantro-Lime Rice

Ingredients

- 2 tbsp. olive oil
- 1 cup white rice (long-grain)
- 1 garlic clove (minced)
- 1 ¼ cups low-sodium chicken broth (or vegetable or water)
- ¼ tsp. fine sea salt (½ if using water)
- ¼ cup chopped cilantro (fresh)
- ½ tsp. grated lime zest (optional)
- 2 tsp. lime juice (freshly squeezed)

Instructions

1. Select Sauté on the pot and set to "Medium" heat. Add the oil to the inner insert.
2. Add the rice and once it shimmers and flows easily. Stir to combine and cook for about 1 minute or until the garlic is fragrant. Then, add the broth (or water) and salt.
3. Secure the lid, tightly closing the vent to "Seal." Select the "Manual or PRESSURE COOK" program to 7 minutes.
4. When the time is up, quick-release the remaining pressure.
5. Carefully unlock and remove the lid. Then, add the cilantro, lime juice, and lime zest (if using). Stir gently to combine.
6. Cover back but don't lock and allow it to sit for 3 to 4 minutes.
7. Fluff with a fork and serve

Yield: 4 servings.

Tomato Rice

Ingredients (for whole spices)

- 1 tsp. cumin seeds
- 1 bay leaf
- 4 cloves
- 2 - 3 pieces cinnamon
- 2 green cardamom pods

Ingredients (main)

- 2 - 3 tbsps. oil (ghee or butter can be used instead)
- 2 tbsps. cashews (optional)
- 4 green chilies (to taste)
- 2 tsps. coriander powder
- 1 tbsp. ginger-garlic paste
- 1 small onion (thinly sliced)
- Red chili powder (to taste)
- 3 - 4 small tomatoes (finely chopped)
- ¼ tsp. turmeric powder
- Salt to taste
- 2 cups rice
- 3 cups of water
- Cilantro (to garnish)

Instructions

1. Start the Instant pot on "Sauté" mode and set on "High". Add oil and once hot, add all the ingredients for spices. Sauté for 2 or 3 minutes to fragrant.
2. Add onions, cashews, and green chili. Continue sautéing for 3 minutes or until onions golden.
3. Add the ginger/garlic paste and continue frying for another 1 minute. Then add tomatoes and sauté for about 5 minutes or until they are mushy.
4. Add the coriander powder, red chili powder, salt, and turmeric powder and mix well.
5. Pour in the rice with water and mix gently. Select "Cancel" to stop sautéing. Tightly lock the lid and shift the vent valve to "Sealing". Then hit the "Rice" button.
6. After the timer counts down to zero, do a quick pressure release after about 4 minutes in warm mode or allow the natural pressure release.
7. Serve hot, garnishing with cilantro and yogurt raita.

Yield: 3 - 4 servings.

Cabbage Rice

Ingredients

- 2 cups Basmati rice
- 2 tbsps. oil
- ¼ tsp. asafetida (optional)
- 1 tsp. mustard seeds
- 4 green chilies (minced)
- Curry leaves (15-20)
- ½ cup peanuts
- ½ tsp. turmeric
- 6 cups of water
- 2 tbsps. ginger(grated)
- 8 cups cabbage (shredded, packed)
- 2 tsps. salt
- 2 tbsps. lemon juice
- ½ cup cilantro (chopped)
- 3 tbsps. fresh coconut (grated)

Instructions

1. Rinse the rice 4 to 5 times. Then soak for about 2 hours in 4 cups of lukewarm water or for 3 hours in cold water. Drain and keep aside.
2. Start the Instant Pot on "Sauté or More" mode. Once the message "Hot" shows on the display panel, add oil and asafetida (if using), and then, the mustard seeds. Allow all of allow them to pop.
3. Add peanuts and keep sautéing for a minute more and add curry leaves, ginger, green chili, and turmeric and cook until peanuts turn golden brown.
4. Add cabbage and salt and stir again.
5. Add the drained rice and stir gently to mix everything together. Then add 2 cups of water.
6. Tightly lock the lid and shift the vent valve to "Sealing". Then hit the "Rice" button.
7. After the timer counts down to zero, allow the natural pressure release and open the Instant Pot when all the pressure has dispersed. Pour in lemon juice.
8. Serve hot garnished with cilantro and coconut.

Yield: 8 servings.

Sweet Coconut Rice

Ingredients

- 4 cups of water
- 1 cup Basmati rice
- 1 tsp. saffron
- 1 tbsp. warm milk
- Whole cashews (15 - 20)
- 2 tbsps. ghee (or coconut, oil divided)
- 2 whole green cardamom pods
- 6 cloves
- 1 tsp. cardamom powder
- 1 cup fresh coconut (grated, frozen is okay)
- 2 tbsps. raisins
- ½ tsp. salt
- ¾ cup sugar

Instructions

1. Rinse the rice a couple of times. Then soak for about 20 minutes in 2 ½ cups lukewarm water or about 40 minutes in cold water. Drain and set aside.
2. Soak the saffron also in warm milk and set aside, for garnishing.
3. Start the Instant Pot on "Sauté or More" mode. Add cashews and 1 tablespoon of ghee oil. Sauté the cashews for 1 minute for them to turn golden brown. Keep stirring constantly. Remove the cashews and set aside for garnishing later.
4. Pour the remaining ghee to the Instant Pot and add cardamom pods and cloves. Cook for about 20 seconds or until fragrant.
5. Add drained rice and gently toast for 1 minute, stirring constantly.
6. Add the salt and the remaining 1½ cups of water. Mix well and ensure that the rice is completely submerged under the water. Tightly close the Instant Pot, locking the lid and setting the pressure release valve to "Sealing". Cook on "Manual/High" for 7 minutes. When the cook time is up, do the natural pressure release for 5 minutes.
7. Unlatch to open the pot. Then add cloves, coconut, raisins, sugar, and cardamom powder. Mix well.
8. Then return the Instant Pot to "Sauté/Less" mode and cook unlocked for 5 minutes but with a glass lid on.
9. Serve, garnished with saffron and fried cashews and enjoy!

Yield: 6 servings.

CHAPTER 5: BEANS RECIPES

The beans cooked in the Instant Pot will share characteristics of other food cooked in the pot. And beans are a flexible food that goes with just about anything. They are good as the main course, not bad as a side. Beans soup is also supper. Here are some ideas about how you can make your beans in your Instant Pot.

Red Beans Coconut Popsicles Recipe

Ingredients

- 8 ½ oz. adzuki beans (red beans)
- 5 cups cold water
- 2 ½ to 3 ½ pieces of cubes rock sugar
- 1 ½ cup tbsp. coconut milk
- 1 ½ tbsp. cornstarch
- 2 tbsp. water

Instruction

1. Rinse beans under cold running tap water. Drain well.
2. Pour the beans inside the Instant Pot and add water. Tightly close the lid and cook at "High Pressure" for 20 minutes.
3. Then turn off the heat and do natural pressure release for 15 minutes and manually release the remaining pressure, carefully turning the knob to the venting position. Open the lid carefully.
4. Press "Sauté" button and add the brown rock sugar. Allow the sugar to melt and the mixture to boil for about 10 minutes. Stir occasionally. Add the coconut milk.
5. Combine the cornstarch with water and add to the adzuki beans mixture gradually in one-third batches. Then turn off the heat.
6. Pour the adzuki beans mixture into a large mixing bowl and allow it to cool.
7. Freeze for 6 hours and then serve.

Yield: 6 servings.

Flavorful Refried Beans

Ingredients
- 4 cups cooked pinto beans (rinse very well and drain the beans completely if you are using canned beans and reserve the liquid)
- 1 ½ tbsp. olive oil
- 1 small yellow onion (diced)
- 5 cloves garlic (minced)
- 2 tsp. paprika
- ½ tsp. chili powder
- ½ tsp. black pepper
- 2 tsp. salt (reduce to 1 teaspoon or avoid if you are using canned beans)
- 2 ½ tsp. cumin
- 1 or 2 pinches of red pepper flakes
- Bean broth (the reserved cooking liquid)

Instructions
1. Fill the Instant Pot with water to submerge the beans for about 2 inches and tightly cover. Check to be sure that the pressure release valve is pushed to the back.
2. Press the Bean/Chili button. This displays 25 minutes on the display of the Instant Pot. The pot should start on its own and will gradually reach the right pressure before the timer begins to count.
3. When it stops, allow natural pressure release and free the remaining pressure. Then do a quick release. Take the lid off.
4. Place a colander on a bowl that is deep enough to contain all the liquid from the beans and pour the beans into the colander. Allow 5 minutes for all liquid to drain into the bowl to be used later.
5. Return the inner insert of the Instant Pot and add the olive oil.
6. Push the Sauté button and add the onion, then stir for 6-7 minutes or until translucent. Add garlic, stir for 1 more minute.
7. Add beans and all of the spices together with the reserved broth. Add more broth to achieve the desired tenderness.
8. Cook for about 10 minutes.
9. Add more salt as needed and serve. You may serve in a tortilla shell or alongside lettuce and rice to make a full meal.

Yield: 3 servings.

Common Baked Beans

Ingredients

- 1 ½ cups cannellini beans (or other beans, dried)
- 1 oz. dried porcini mushrooms (or shiitake mushrooms)
- 1 cup of warm water
- 2 tbsp. olive oil
- 1 medium or large brown onion (finely diced)
- ½ long red chili (optional, diced or sliced)
- ¼ teaspoon salt
- 2 cloves of garlic (finely diced)
- 1 medium carrot (diced into small cubes)
- 1 can of chopped tin tomatoes (or tomato paste)
- 1 tbsp. soy sauce (or tamari sauce)
- 1 tbsp. ketchup
- 2 tbsp. brown sugar
- 1 onion stock cube (or 2 tbsp. of onion soup mix)
- 1 tsp. smoked paprika (or 1 ½ of regular paprika)
- ½ teaspoon allspice powder
- 2 bay leaves

Instructions

1. Pour water onto the dried beans inside a large bowl and mix in a teaspoon of salt. Soak for a minimum of 8 hours then rinse and strain.
2. Soak the porcini mushrooms for 10-20 minutes in a cup of warm water to rehydrate.
3. Turn the Instant Pot to the "Sauté" function and add the chili, olive oil, and onions. Cook for 5 minutes and stir a couple of time.
4. Remove the mushrooms (but keep the water), then chop into small pieces.
5. Cook for minutes and stir in the remaining ingredients, beans, mushrooms, and the reserved mushroom liquid, then select "Keep Warm/Cancel."
6. Tightly lock the lid. Set the pot to "Manual or High Pressure", and timer for 12 minutes.
7. Once it beeps three times, the Instant Pot will start building up the pressure and begin cooking. (If the beans are not soaked, cook for 35 minutes.)
8. Once the timer beeps to go off, allow natural pressure release for about 10-15 minutes. Then open the lid and stir and serve.
9. You can refrigerate for 3 - 4 days.

Yield: 4 - 6 servings.

Chili With Dry Beans

Ingredients

- 6 cups water
- 3 cups dry pinto beans
- 1 lb. ground beef
- 1 lb. ground pork sausage
- 3 cans diced tomatoes (14 ½ oz. each)
- 1 can tomato sauce (14 ½ oz.)
- 1 can green chili (diced, roasted 7 oz.)
- 3 tbsp. chili powder
- 1 onion (diced)
- 1 cup beef broth
- 1 green bell pepper (diced)
- 6 cloves garlic (minced or 3 tsp.)
- 1½ tbsp. cumin
- 1 tbsp. paprika
- ½ tbsp. black pepper
- ½ tbsp. oregano
- 1 tbsp. sea salt

Instructions

1. Rinse and sort pinto beans and add to clean Instant Pot liner. Then add water and close the lid, making sure that the vent valve is shut.
2. Press the "Bean/Chili" button and set the timer to 20 minutes. Meanwhile, mix other ingredients like bell pepper and onion.
3. Once the timer beeps, allow 10 minutes of natural pressure release and flip vent to allow the pin to drop. Then open the lid.
4. Drain the beans and clean the pot (you may wipe it). Then, press the "Sauté" button, wait until it gets to "Hot". Then, add 1 tbsp. vegetable oil, then ground beef and sausage. Cook and divide until browned. Once browned, use a mesh strainer to drain the meat.
5. Return meat to the pot, add onion and bell pepper and cook for a few minutes. Add the garlic and cook for 1 or 2 more minutes. Add both diced tomatoes and tomato sauce and all seasonings. Then, return the beans to the pot and stir.
6. Tightly close lid and have vent valve shut. Then press the "Bean/Chili" and set the timer for 20 minutes.
7. After 20 minutes, naturally release the pressure for 10 minutes and adjust the vent valve to release the remaining pressure until pin drops. Open, stir, and serve.

Yield: 4 servings.

Moroccan-Style Chickpea Stew

Ingredients

- 1 large onion (chopped)
- 2 tbsp. olive oil
- 5 cloves of garlic (finely chopped or crushed)
- 2 tsp. ground cinnamon
- 2 tsp. cumin (ground)
- ¼ tsp. cayenne pepper (chili may be used)
- 2 tsp. paprika (full heap)
- 1 tin of chopped tomatoes (400g)
- 2 tins of chickpeas or garbanzo beans (400 g each, to be well rinsed and drained)
- 2 tbsp. of raisins
- 12 tomatoes (sun-dried, chopped into pieces with a knife or scissors)
- Small 140 g or 5 oz of baby spinach (or a few lumps of spinach, frozen)
- 3 ½ cups vegetable stock (750ml, premade or made with veggie stock)
- ½ tsp. salt and pepper to taste
- Small fresh cilantro (or parsley leaves to serve)

Instructions

1. Start your Instant Pot and select the "Sauté" function. When slightly heated, add the olive oil and onion and cook for 2-3 minutes. Then stir in the garlic and spices and continue cooking for about 30 seconds.
2. Add the remaining ingredients and stir through. Stop sautéing by selecting "Cancel."
3. Tightly close the lid and check to ensure that the steam valve is set at "Sealing." Set the Instant Pot to "Manual/ High" and timer to 10 minutes. The pressure will start to build up and cooking will begin after 3 beeps. Once the timer goes off, wait for 10 minutes for natural pressure release. Do a quick release to allow out the rest of the steam (You do this by switching the sealing valve to "Venting").
4. Open the lid, stir the stew slightly and wait for 5 minutes. Then serve with fresh herbs on top. It can be a nice side for cooked rice, crusty bread, or couscous.

Yield: 3 - 5 servings.

Quick and Easy Hummus

Ingredients

- 1 cup dried chickpeas (garbanzo beans)
- 3 - 4 cups hot water
- ½ teaspoon salt
- 3 cups water
- 1 cube vegetable stock
- 2 tbsp. olive oil
- 3 tbsp. light tahini
- ¼ cup plus 2 tbsp. lemon juice
- 2 cloves of garlic (roughly chopped)
- 1 tsp. cumin powder
- Pinch of salt (or more to taste)
- 1 cup cooking liquid (or require to thin it depending on the size)
- Olive oil to taste and a pinch of paprika and cumin powder

Instructions

1. If you are using the soaking method, in a bowl, add the chickpeas with hot water and salt. Leave for 8 hours and rinse. Then add to the Instant Pot.
2. If you are cooking dried, pour the chickpeas into the water to be submerged inside the Instant Pot. Add the vegetable stock. You can use ready-prepared vegetable stock or break a cube and add.
3. Tightly close the lid and check to ensure that the steam valve is set at "Sealing." Set the Instant Pot to "Manual/ High" for 35 minutes. The pressure will start to build up and cooking will begin after 3 beeps. Once the timer goes off, wait for 5 minutes for natural pressure release. Do a quick release to allow out the rest of the steam. Then, open the lid.
   (The same procedure goes for soaked chickpeas. The only difference is the timer should be set to 25 minutes.)
4. Strain the chickpeas in a bowl to keep with liquid, using a sieve. Add the cumin, garlic, lemon juice, olive oil, tahini, and a little pinch of salt to the cooked chickpeas inside a food processor and add about ½ cup of the liquid. Then, process into thick puree. Scrape the mixture from the sides and repeat the process, adding the rest of the liquid each time until smooth to your desire for immediate or later use.
5. Drizzle with olive oil and a sprinkle with paprika or/and cumin while serving. It can be refrigerated in an airtight container for up to 6 days.

Yield: 2 servings.

Red Beans With Rice

Ingredients

- ½ bell pepper (diced)
- ½ celery stalks (diced)
- ½ cloves garlic (minced)
- ½ medium onion(diced)
- ½ pound red kidney beans (dried)
- ¼ tsp. black pepper
- ¼ tsp. white pepper (optional)
- ½ tsp. hot sauce
- 1 ½ tsp. fresh thyme (or ½ tsp dried thyme)
- 1 bay leaf
- 3 ½ cups water
- ½ pound chicken andouille sausage (cut into thin slices)
- ½ tsp. salt (or as desired)
- 5 cups cooked rice

Instructions

1. Combine all ingredients, except for rice and sausage inside the Instant Pot and tightly cover. Check to ensure that the steam valve is set at "Sealing."
2. Set the Instant Pot to "Manual/ High" for 28 minutes. Once the timer goes off, do the quick release by releasing the valve and allow the Instant Pot is completely depressurized (when the pin falls). Then remove the lid and set aside to cook or run under water.
3. Add the chicken andouille sausage and place the lid on, reseal it.
4. Select "Manual" and set to 15 minutes High Pressure, After cooking this time, allow the natural pressure release; wait for about 15 minutes for the pin to drop.
5. Wait for a few minutes to allow the beans mixture to thicken the liquid.
6. Serve the beans mixture over your rice or any main course.

Yield: 5 servings.

Loaded Baked Beans

Ingredients

- 1 can chili beans (27 oz.)
- 1 can butter beans (16 oz.)
- 1 can bake beans (28 oz.)
- 1 lb. ground beef (ground and drained)
- 1 lb. bacon sliced (cooked and drained)
- 1 tsp. onion powder
- 1 tbsp. garlic 9 (minced)
- ½ cup of ketchup
- 1 tbsp. brown mustard
- ½ cup brown sugar
- 1 tsp. of white vinegar

Instructions

1. Have your hamburger browned up and cook up your bacon. Drain both of grease. (You may spray your Instant Pot with a nonstick spray to prevent sugars from burning and sticking.)
2. Pour all the beans into the crockpot and add in all other ingredients and stir
3. Then, tightly seal up the lead and set the Instant Pot to "Manual/ High" and timer for 7 minutes.
4. Once cooked wait for natural pressure release and serve. Enjoy!

Yield: 2 servings.

Greek Stewed Lima Beans

Ingredients

- 1 cup leek (diced, mostly the white part)
- 4 cloves garlic (minced)
- 1 cup of diced carrot
- ½ tsp. crumbled dried rosemary
- 1 - 2 tsp. dried oregano
- 1¼ cups vegetable stock
- 1 cup baby lima beans (soaked and drained)
- 2 bay leaves
- 1 cup chopped fennel bulb (cut into 1-inch pieces)
- ¼ cup fennel fronds 9 chopped)
- ½ cup frozen artichoke hearts (not thawed or drained canned)
- 1 tsp. grated lemon zest
- 1 - 2 tbsp. lemon juice (fresh)
- ½ tsp. dried mint (or 2 tsp. chopped fresh)
- Salt and black pepper (freshly ground)
- 2 tsp. extra virgin olive oil (optional)
- 1 tbsp. olive oil (optional)

Instructions

1. Set the Instant Pot to "Sauté" and pour the oil. Add your leek and sauté for 2 minutes. Then, add the carrot, garlic, rosemary, and oregano and sauté for a minute more and stir often. Add 1 tablespoon of the stock and stir well to avoid any sticking.
2. Add and combine well the remaining stock with the drained beans, bay leaves, artichoke hearts, fennel bulb, and fronds.
3. Tightly close the lid and check to ensure that the steam valve is set at "Sealing." Set the Instant Pot to "Manual/ High" for 6 minutes. Once the timer goes off, wait for natural pressure release. Then, carefully open the lid.
4. Taste to ensure the beans are cooked through. If you need to, you can cook again on "High Pressure" for 1 to 2 more minutes.
5. Add the mint, lemon zest, and juice. Then, add salt and pepper to taste. If you want, you can add the remaining oregano for a highly flavored dish.
6. Serve and drizzle with extra virgin olive oil.

Yield: 4 servings.

Chili Lime Black Beans

Ingredients

- 2 cups dry black beans (sorted and rinsed)
- 1 onion (chopped)
- 2 tsp. coconut oil
- 4 cloves garlic (fresh)
- 1 tbsp. chili powder
- 1 tsp. smoked paprika
- 2-3 tsp. mineral salt (e.g. pink Himalayan
- 3 cups water (or more for more liquid in the beans)
- Juice of 1 lime

Instructions

1. Set Instant Pot to "Sauté" and add the oil. Allow to melt and then add garlic and onion. Next, sauté for 3 minutes.
2. Add water, beans, smoked paprika chili powder, and salt.
3. Tightly close the lid and check to ensure that the steam valve is set at "Sealing." Set the Instant Pot to "Manual" for 50 minutes.
4. Once the timer goes off, wait for natural pressure release. Then, carefully open the lid and add lime juice and stir well.
5. Taste and adjust seasonings to the desired taste. Then serve.

Yield: 6 servings.

Spicy Black Bean Dip

Ingredients (dry)

- 1 tbsp. chili powder
- 2 tsps. cumin (ground)
- 1 tbsp. smoked paprika
- 1 tsp. sea salt
- 1 tsp. dried garlic
- ¼ cup onion (dried)
- 2 tbsps. green bell pepper (dried)
- 2 cups black beans (dried)

Ingredients (for cooking and serving)

- 3 ½ cups vegetable broth (or water; you may add more as needed)
- ¼ cup mozzarella cheese (to serve; shredded; optional)
- Green bell peppers (diced; to serve)
- Red onion (diced; to serve)
- Corn chips (or raw vegetables; for dipping)

Instructions

1. Prepare by layering all the dry ingredients in a jar in the listed order.
2. Begin to cook by placing all the jarred ingredients into your Instant Pot. Add the water or 3 ½ cups of vegetable broth. Stir well to mix. Tightly cover with the lid. Make sure that the pressure release knob is shifted to the "Sealed" position. Then, select the "Pressure Cook or Manual" and cook on High pressure for 35 minutes.
3. After the cooking time, allow 20 minutes for the natural pressure release. Then insert an immersion blender to purée the beans mixture until the desired smoothness. Alternatively, you can transfer it into the bowl of a standing blender. You may add more water or vegetable broth as needed while blending.
4. To serve, pour the smooth mixture into a serving dish. If using, top with the cheese, peppers, and onions.
5. Then serve with raw vegetables or corn chips.

Yield: 6 - 8 servings.

CHAPTER 6: EGGS RECIPES

If for the protein contents of the egg alone, it can't be easily removed from diets and cuisines. Regardless of the method and equipment of cooking, the egg will always stand out. Any discussion about the Instant Pot will not be fair if it has not explored eggs recipes. Consider the 10 meals you can make with eggs on your Instant Pot.

The Instant Pot Egg Bites

Ingredients
- 8 large eggs
- ¼ cup milk
- ¼ tsp. salt
- 1/8 tsp. black pepper (freshly ground)
- ½ cup diced ham (or precooked bacon or both)
- 1/3 cup cheddar cheese (shredded)
- 1 green onion (optional)
- I cup of water

Instructions
1. Spray plenty nonstick cooking spray on two silicone baby food trays. Then combine the eggs, milk, pepper, and salt in a large bowl. Whisk until they are well blended. Then divide the ham equally into the silicone cups. Pour the egg mixture over the meat into the cups until they are two thirds full and sprinkle the shredded cheese over the egg bites.
2. Position the trivet in the bottom of the Instant Pot and water. Lower each silicone trays using a sling by stacking them carefully on top of the other. Tightly lock the lid and select "High Pressure" and set the cook timer to 11 minutes for the eggs bite to become firm. Reduce the time if you want less firm eggs.
3. Turn off the Instant Pot when the cook time ends and allow natural pressure release for 5 minutes. Then do a quick pressure release and until the release valve drops, remove the lid carefully and remove the trays using the sling. Place the tray on a wire rack for 5 minutes to cool down.
4. Carefully turn the tray over and squeeze gently to remove the egg bites.
5. Slice the egg bites or serve on top of toast or mini croissants.

Yield: 14 servings.

The Instant Pot Egg Muffins

Ingredients:

- 4 eggs (medium to large)
- ¼ tsp. lemon-pepper seasoning
- 4 tbsp. cheddar/Jack cheese (shredded)
- 1 green onion (diced)
- 4 slices precooked bacon, crumbled
- 1 ½ cups of water

Instructions:

1. Pour little water on the Instant Pot and put the steamer basket inside.
2. Whisk well the eggs with pour spout in a large measuring bowl adding the lemon pepper. Divide the bacon, cheese, and green onion fairly equally inside four silicone muffin cups. Fill each muffin cup with the whisked eggs to cover over the ingredients inside the cup. Combine by stirring with a fork.
3. Place each muffin cup on the steamer basket and tightly lock the lid and select "High Pressure" and set the cook timer to 2 minutes. Turn off the Instant Pot when the cook time ends and do a quick pressure release. Remove the lid carefully lift the steamer basket out to remove the muffins.
4. Serve immediately. The muffins can be refrigerated up to two weeks and reheated.

Yield: 2 servings.

Zesty Deviled Eggs

Ingredients

- 6 hard-boiled eggs
- 1 ½ tbsp. of mayonnaise
- 1 ½ tbsp. of low-fat Greek yogurt
- 1 ½ tsp. jalapeno mustard
- ¼ tsp. onion powder
- Kosher salt and black pepper (freshly ground, to taste).
- Paprika (for sprinkling as toppings)
- 2 tsp. barbecue sauce (optional)
- 1/8 tsp. garlic powder

Instructions

1. Cut the egg in half and put yolks in a medium bowl.
2. Mash the yolks with a fork and add Greek yogurt, jalapeno mustard, and mayonnaise. Using hand mixer beat all together until smooth.
3. Stir in the onion powder and season with salt and pepper to taste.
4. If you feel that you need a little more mustard, add a little more and mix everything again. Also, add a little of either mayonnaise or yogurt if it still looks a little dry. This depends on the size of the eggs used.
5. Use a spoon or pipe to pour the yolk mixture into the half egg white hollow and sprinkle lightly with paprika as toppings.

Yield: 3 servings.

Bacon Barbecue Deviled Eggs

Ingredients
- 8 hard-boiled eggs
- 1 ½ tbsp. plus 1 tsp. low-fat Greek yogurt
- 1 ½ tbsp. plus 1 tsp. mayonnaise
- ¼ tsp. onion powder
- 4-5 slices bacon
- 1 ½ tsp. yellow mustard
- 2 ½ tsp. barbecue sauce
- 1/8 tsp. garlic powder
- ¼ tsp. onion powder
- Kosher salt and black pepper (freshly ground, to taste).

Instructions
1. In a large non-stick skillet, cook the bacon until it turns crisp. Then, drain the slices of bacon on paper towels. When cooled, finely chop, set aside.
2. Slice each egg in half and place their yolks in a medium bowl and mash with a fork.
3. Then add the barbecue sauce, Greek yogurt, mayonnaise, and yellow mustard.
4. Using a hand mixer beat all ingredients until smooth, stir in the garlic powder and onion powder.
5. Season with pepper and kosher salt to taste and stir in half of the bacon.
6. Use a spoon or pipe to pour the yolk mixture into the half egg white hollow and sprinkle the remaining bacon as toppings.

Yield: 4 servings.

Crustless Meat Lovers Quiche

Ingredients

- 6 large eggs, well beaten
- ½ cup milk
- 1/8 tsp. black pepper (ground)
- 4 slices bacon (cooked and crumbled)
- 1 cup cooked sausage (ground)
- ½ cup of diced ham
- 2 large green onions (chopped)
- 1 cup cheese (shredded)
- 1 cup of water
- ¼ tsp. salt

Instructions

1. Lower a trivet into the bottom of the Instant Pot, and then add 1 cup water.
2. Whisk the eggs, milk, pepper, and salt together in a large bowl and set aside.
3. Mix together bacon, cheese, green onions, ham, and sausage inside a 1-quart soufflé dish.
4. Stir in the egg mixture with the meat to combine.
5. Cover the soufflé dish (not too tightly) with aluminum foil. Let the soufflé dish be on the center of a foil sling. Carefully lower onto the trivet inside the Instant Pot
6. Tightly lock the cooking pot.
7. Set the Instant Port to "High Pressure", set the timer to 30 minutes.
8. When the timer stops, wait for 10 minutes for natural pressure release and then do a quick pressure release for the valve to drop.
9. Carefully open the lid and lift out the soufflé dish to remove the foil.
10. Sprinkle additional cheese on the top of the quiche. Broil to bring to melt and brown.
11. Then serve immediately.

Yield: 4 servings.

Crustless Tomato Spinach Quiche

Ingredients
- 12 large eggs
- ½ cup milk
- ¼ tsp. black pepper (fresh, ground)
- 3 cups fresh baby spinach (roughly chopped)
- 1 cup tomato (diced, seeded)
- 3 large green onions (sliced)
- 4 tomato slices (for topping the quiche)
- ¼ cup Parmesan cheese (shredded)
- 1 ½ cups of water
- ½ tsp. salt

Instructions
1. Lower a metal trivet into the bottom of the Instant Pot, and then add 1 ½ cup of water.
2. Whisk together the eggs, milk, pepper, and salt in a large bowl. Combine well green onions, spinach, and tomato, with 1 ½ quart-size baking dish. Then pour the egg mixture over the veggies; stir well to combine properly. Place the sliced tomatoes on top gently and sprinkle with the cheese.
3. Using a sling, place the dish on the trivet inside the Instant Pot and tightly lock. Then select "High Pressure," set the timer to 20 minutes and start cooking.
4. When timer beeps and cooking stops, allow natural pressure release for 10 minutes and then do a quick release.
5. Open the lid carefully and lift out the dish. Broil to bring to brown lightly, if desired.
6. Serve immediately, topped with tomato slices.

Yield: 6 servings.

Perfect Hard-Boiled and Soft-Boiled Eggs

Ingredients

- 2 to 4 large eggs
- 1 cup of water

Instructions

1. Place the egg rack or steaming rack in the Instant Pot. Place your egg on the rack in such a way that they won't have direct contact with the side of your pot. Then pour 1 cup water into the pot (it should go to the bottom ideally).
2. Tightly close the lid ensuring that the valve is sealed. Select the "Manual" button and set the pressure to "High" and the timer to correspond to the preferred results. (Set it to 3 minutes if you want perfect soft-boiled eggs, 5 minutes if you want medium eggs, and 8 minutes if you prefer hard-boiled eggs).
3. Get ready for ice bathing by preparing a few handfuls of ice cubes or blocks and some water in a big bowl.
4. When you hear the beep indicating that the cooking is completed, do quick pressure release immediately by using a pair of tongs to turn the valve. The pressure will release in 60 seconds, maximum, and you will hear a click.
5. Open the lid immediately and use the tongs to transfer your eggs into the ice bath.
6. Allow it to cool for 1 to 2 minutes so that you can safely and comfortably handle the egg.
7. Then, peels the eggs and serve in a plate. (It can also be stored in an airtight container for up to 4 days in the fridge.)

Serving: 1 large serving.

Chinese Yellow Chives and Eggs Stir Fry

Ingredients

- 1 small batch (14 oz. or 400g) Chinese yellow chives
- 4 large eggs (beaten)
- 1 ½ tbsp. vegetable oil (or peanut oil)
- ½ tsp. salt

Instructions

1. Under running water, rinse the yellow chives while using your fingers to gently wash each of them in small batches to wash off all dirt and removed peel off any withered parts and ends.
2. Then, drain the chives and chop (about 2 inches from the bottom part. So discard the tough white part).
3. Chop the remaining chives into 2-inch pieces and set aside.
4. Heat ½ tablespoon of the oil in a large 12 inches nonstick skillet over "Medium-High" and bring to warm.
5. Add the eggs and allow them to cook until the bottom sets. Keep stirring and chopping with a spatula so that you will have smaller bits as you would if making scrambled eggs.
6. After cooking, remove the pan from inside the pot and transfer the eggs to a plate.
7. Add the remaining 1 tablespoon of oil and leave for about 60 seconds when the oil would have started to smoke. Then add the yellow chives and start stirring immediately for a few times so that oil will coat the chives properly.
8. Return the eggs into Instant Pot when the chive is tender and sprinkle everything with evenly with salt. Continue stirring and cooking until the chives turn tender completely and the volume reduces.
9. Once done, transfer all into a plate and serve hot immediately maybe over steamed rice or another course.

Yield: 2 servings.

Sausage Egg Casserole

Ingredients

- 8 large eggs
- 6 turkey breakfast sausages (cooked and sliced)
- 1 ½ cups of water
- ½ cup milk
- ½ tsp. parsley
- ½ cup shredded cheddar cheese (divided)
- 3/4 cup hashbrowns (frozen)
- 1 green onion (sliced)
- 1/8 tsp. pepper
- 3/4 tsp. salt

Instructions

1. Whisk together eggs, milk, parsley, pepper, and salt in a large bowl or large glass measuring cup.
2. Lightly grease your baking dish.
3. Add ¼ cup of cheese, green onion, hash browns, and sausages in layers inside the baking dish.
4. Pour the whisked eggs on top and sprinkle with the other ¼ cup of cheese.
5. Pour 1 ½ cups of water into your Instant Pot. Cover the baking dish with foil and lower into the trivet inside the Instant Pot.
6. Tightly close the lid, ensuring that it's turned to sealing.
7. Select "Manual or Pressure Cook" and set the timer for 35 minutes. (It takes about 10 minutes for the pressure to build up).
8. When the timer for beeps to indicate that the cooking is done, allow the pressure to naturally release for about 10 minutes. Then, open the valve to remove the lid. Take the baking dish out of the pressure cooker and serve the egg immediately.

Yield: 4 servings.

Cheesy Eggs

Ingredients

- 6 slices bacon (chopped)
- 2 cups hash browns (frozen)
- 6 large eggs
- 1 ½ cups of water
- ¼ cup milk
- ½ cup cheddar cheese (shredded)
- ½ tsp. pepper
- 1 tsp. salt
- green onions, mushrooms, onion, red pepper, and spinach (optional add-ins, as desired)

Instructions

1. Chop bacon into small pieces and add to the Instant Pot. Set to "Sauté" to crispy.
2. Add extra veggies of your choice and sauté until tender, which takes about 3 minutes.
3. Add frozen hash browns and stir slightly to bring to thaw, which takes about two minutes.
4. Grease a 1 ½-quart heatproof casserole dish or any other one that fits well into your Instant Pot.
5. Whisk together eggs, shredded cheese, milk, pepper, and salt in a separate bowl. Then add bacon and veggie mixture from the Instant Pot and combine everything into a prepared heatproof casserole dish.
6. Set the trivet inside the Instant Pot and pour water to go to the bottom of the pot. Place a heatproof bowl containing all the ingredients on the trivet.
7. Tightly close the lid ensuring that the valve is sealed. Select the "Manual" button and set the pressure to "High" and the timer to 20 minutes. When the cooking is done, do a quick release of the pressure.
8. Remove the casserole dish from the Instant Pot carefully and loosen the edges with a knife. Then, pour into a large plate. You can also serve directly from the dish with the remaining shredded cheese and green onions.

Yield: 4 servings.

Bacon and Asiago Egg Bites

Ingredients

- 4 eggs
- ¾ cup asiago cheese (shredded)
- ½ cup cottage cheese
- ¼ cup heavy cream
- ½ tsp. salt
- ¼ tsp. pepper
- 1 dash hot sauce (optional)
- 4 strips bacon (cooked and crumbled)

Instructions

1. Combine the other 7 ingredients, except the bacon, in a blender. Puree into a smooth mixture for about 15 seconds.
2. Coat the silicone egg mold in the inside with nonstick spray.
3. Distribute the bacon evenly into the egg molds. Then pour smooth mixture evenly on the bacon in each mold and loosely cover with foil.
4. Pour one cup of water in the Instant Pot and insert the steam rack.
5. Carefully lower the mold onto the steam rack inside the pot. Tightly secure the lid, ensuring that the vent valve is closed.
6. On the display panel, press "Manual or Pressure Cook." Use the +/- keys button to program the Instant Pot to 10 minutes of cooking.
7. When the pot beeps to indicate the end of cooking, do a quick release of the pressure.
8. Open and take the egg mold out and allow it to cool for 2-3 minutes. Unmold the egg bites and enjoy immediately. You can refrigerate for up to one week.

Yield: 4 servings.

CHAPTER 7: CHICKEN RECIPES

What have you not tried with the chicken before? Is it whole chicken or exciting chicken soups? You have seen breasts and wings made into all sorts of delicacies. However, you are still missing out on some potential tastes of chicken meals if you have not cooked it in the Instant Pot. Meanwhile, it can do EVERYTHING you can ever think of about chicken. Here are a few of the popular chicken recipes to inspire your cooking.

Buffalo Chicken Wings

Ingredients

- 3 lbs. ice glazed chicken wings (not-breaded, frozen individually, if possible)
- ¼ cup chicken broth
- ½ cup red hot sauce
- 4 tbsps. butter (to be cut into two or three pieces, ½ stick)
- 2 tbsps. Cajun seasoning blend (dried)
- 2 oz. blue cheese (crumbled, ½ cup)
- ½ cup mayonnaise (regular or low-fat)
- ½ cup sour cream (regular or low-fat)
- ½ tsp. onion powder
- ½ tsp. black pepper (ground)

Instructions

1. Combine the broth, butter, hot sauce, and seasoning blend in your Instant Pot to make a sauce. Set in the wings and toss well.
2. Tightly lock the lid and set the pot to "Maximum Pressure" and the timer to 12 minutes.
3. Another option is to press "Poultry" function and pressure on "Manual High" for 15 minutes. Let the "Warm" setting be off. Then quick release the pressure and open the cooker. Transfer the wings into a large platter.
4. Whisk the blue cheese, mayonnaise, onion powder, and pepper together with the sour cream in a small bowl.
5. Serve the hot wings with the creamy sauce as a dip. You can also use the boiled down liquid fetched from the pot as another dip.

Yield: 4 - 6 servings.

Chicken Teriyaki

Ingredients

- 3 lbs. frozen chicken thighs (boneless and skinless)
- 3/4 cup chicken broth
- ½ cup frozen chopped onion (or 1 small white or yellow onion, to be peeled and chopped)
- 3 tbsps. light brown sugar
- 2 tbsps. fresh ginger (peeled and minced)
- 1 tbsp. garlic (peeled and minced)
- ½ cup regular soy sauce or tamari (or reduced-sodium)

Instructions

1. Combine the broth, brown sugar, garlic, ginger, onion, and soy sauce or tamari in an Instant Pot and add the chunks or block chicken and stir well.
2. Tightly lock the lid and set the pot to "Maximum Pressure" and the timer to 17 minutes, keeping "Warm" setting off.
3. Once the machine beeps after cooking, wait for about 25 minutes to allow natural pressure release before unlatching the lid to open the cooker. Then transfer the chicken thighs into a bowl.
4. Select "Sauté" function and set it to "High" "More" or to 400°F with the timer on 15 minutes and press "Start."
5. Bring the sauce to boil in the pot. Keep stirring often as it continues boiling until the sauce becomes a thick glaze, which takes about 7 minutes. Then, stop the "Sauté" function and return the chicken thighs and juices to the pot. Keep stirring until the glaze coats the chicken. Serve hot in a platter or serving plates.

Yield: 6 servings.

Chicken Fajitas

Ingredients

- 1 large onion (peeled, halved, and sliced thinly into half-moons)
- 3/4 cup chicken broth
- 12 oz. fajita seasoning (1 package)
- 2 tbsps. pickled jalapeño rings (with some of the pickling juice)
- 2 lbs. frozen chicken tenders
- 1 lb. frozen bell pepper strips (4 cups)

Instructions

1. In an Instant Pot, combine well the slices of onion with the broth, jalapeño rings and juice, and half of the seasoning blend.
2. Set the rack of the pot (handles up) or a large vegetable steamer in the mixture.
3. Arrange the half of the chicken on the rack and sprinkle with remaining half of the seasoning blend.
4. Then, top with the other chicken tenders. Sprinkle with the remaining seasoning.
5. Top with the bell pepper strips without stirring or tossing.
6. Tightly lock the lid and set the pot to "Maximum Pressure" and the timer to 12 minutes, keeping "Warm" setting off.
7. Once the timer beeps after cooking, do a quick release and allow the pressure to escape. Unlatch the lid to open the cooker and use cooking mitts or kitchen tongs to move out the rack or steamer from the pot. Pour the chicken into the sauce below and stir well.
8. Press the "Sauté" button and set the pot to "High," "More," or "Custom 400°F" with the timer set to 15 minutes.
9. When it is done, using a slotted spoon, transfer the chicken tenders with the whole vegetables to a large plate.
10. Bring the sauce to boil by stirring often for about 10 minutes or until it turns to a glaze. Then stop the "Sauté" and pour the sauce evenly over the chicken and vegetables.
11. Then serve immediately!

Yield: 6 servings.

Road Map: Bone-In Chicken Breasts

Ingredients

- 1 cup of water (or broth; you may also choose liquid of any sort from brands and types of wine, beer, unsweetened apple cider. You may also combine any of these)
- 12-14 oz. bone-in skin-on chicken breasts (about 6 frozen pieces)
- 2 tbsps. dried seasoning blend.
- 1 ½ tsps. table salt (optional, if the seasoning blend doesn't include salt)

Instructions
1. Carefully position the bone-in chicken in the water or broth inside the Instant Pot in a crisscross pattern (not stacking on each other). This allows steam to circulate. Then sprinkle their tops with half of both the seasoning blend and of table salt (if using)
2. Tightly lock the lid and set the pot to "Maximum Pressure" and the timer to 35 minutes, keeping "Warm" setting off. Once the timer beeps after cooking, do a quick release and allow the pressure back to normal.
3. Unlatch the lid to open the cooker and check the breasts' internal temperature to be sure that it is 165°F. (There is an instant-read-meat thermometer for this purpose that you can insert into the center of one or two breasts without touching the bone). It is not safe to eat unless the temperature is 165°F. (Though it is okay with the temperature, you may want to cook for 3 or 4 more minutes on "Max" or "High" if there is a little pink that you are not yet comfortable with.)
4. Once the timer beeps after cooking, do a quick release and allow all the pressure to return to normal. Then serve in plates using kitchen tongs. (You may allow them cool to at room temperature for 25 minutes and refrigerate in an airtight container for up to 3 days and reheat.

Yield: 6 servings.

Vortex Plus Parmesan Chicken Fingers

Ingredients

- 1 lb. chicken tenders (about 8 pieces)
- ½ cup flour
- ¼ tsp. pepper
- ¾ cup panko breadcrumbs
- 2 eggs (beaten)
- 1 tsp. Italian seasoning
- ¾ cup parmesan cheese (finely grated)
- 1 tsp. kosher salt
- Marinara honey mustard for dipping (optional, or ranch)

Instructions

1. Combine flour, pepper, and salt in a shallow dish. Have a second one for beaten eggs, and yet another one for breadcrumbs, Italian seasoning, and parmesan cheese. The three dishes will be dredging.
2. Dredge each chicken tender in each of the mixtures in each of the dishes one after the other while pressing the crumbs firmly on both sides in the third shallow dish.
3. Now set the coated chicken onto the cooking tray; allow few inches gap for steaming and put another tray at the bottom to collect drippings.
4. Fry in the cooking chamber and with the temperature of 360°F and the timer set at 15 minutes.
5. When the pot beeps to indicate the end of cooking, quick release the pressure and wait.
6. Remove the tender and serve with the dripping as the sauce.

Yield: 2 - 4 servings.

Chicken Pesto Roll-Up

Ingredients

- ½ cup chicken broth
- 2 lbs. chicken breasts (about 4 breasts)
- ¼ cup pesto (jarred)
- 2 oz. mozzarella (or provolone) cheese
- 1 medium tomato (thinly sliced)
- 1 tbsp. butter
- 1 tbsp. olive oil
- 1 cup panko bread crumbs
- 2 tbsp. grated parmesan
- ½ cup marinara sauce (warmed)
- 2 tbsps. fresh basil (cut into ribbons) for garnish
- pepper
- kosher salt

Instructions

1. Pour the broth into your Instant Pot and place the smooth side of the chicken breasts inside the Instant Pot between two plastic wrap sheets. Pound until it is about ¼ inch thick.
2. Evenly spread the pesto, cheese, and sliced tomatoes one after the other and sprinkle with pepper and salt to taste.
3. Roll up each breast from the one short end and place each bundle seam inside the Instant Pot side down.
4. Tightly close the lid and set the pot to "Manual" or "Pressure Cook" and set the timer to 5 minutes. Once the timer beeps after cooking, allow the natural pressure release for another 5 minutes and do a quick release of the remaining pressure.
5. In the meantime, in a nonstick skillet, heat olive oil and butter. Add panko, parmesan, and a little salt to and pepper grinds to taste.
6. Keep stirring constantly as you start to cook until it turns golden brown. Take the heat out and continue stirring for 30 seconds.
7. Once the cooking is complete, take the roll-ups out of the pot and dip each of them in the skillet so that the bottom is coated with a toasted crumb. Then serve with the sprinkle of remaining crumbs as the topping of the roll-ups. Also, drizzle with marinara together with basil ribbons.

Yield: 4 servings.

Apricot Pineapple Chicken Thighs

Ingredients

- 2 tbsps. vegetable oil
- 6 chicken thighs (skin and visible fat removed)
- ½ cup apricot pineapple jam
- 2 tbsps. soy sauce
- 1 cup of water

Instructions

1. Set the Instant Pot to "High Sauté" heat for a few minutes. Add oil and after about 30 seconds, 3 of the chicken thighs pot and cook each side (for 3 minutes) until each side turns golden brown. Do the same with the remaining thighs. Then select "Cancel" to end sautéing.
2. Whisk together the soy sauce and jam and in a medium bowl and toss to have them coat the jam. Add water into the pot and put the wire trivet and arrange thighs on top of it. Tightly lock the lid set to "Pressure Cook" or "Manual" on "High Pressure" while the timer is set for 20 minutes. Allow it sit for 10 minutes for "Natural Pressure Release" and then do a Quick Pressure Release.
3. Set the thighs in a serving plate. Then, set the pot "High Sauté" and allow 5 minutes for the liquid to simmer and thicken while whisking frequently. Serve with a drizzle of thickened sauce.

Yield: 6 servings.

Indian Butter Chicken

Ingredients

- ½ cup whole raw cashews
- 6 tbsps. ghee (or unsalted grass-fed butter)
- 3 lbs. boneless skinless chicken thighs (trimmed of fat, cut into 2-inch cubes)
- 2 shallots (chopped to fill about ½ cup)
- 1 cup tomato puree
- ¾ cup tomato paste
- 3 tbsps. lemon juice (freshly squeezed)
- 4 cloves garlic (minced)
- 6 green cardamom pods (bruised with the butt of a knife)
- ½ yellow onion (chopped)
- 2 bay leaves
- 3 tbsps. ginger (peeled and minced)
- 2 ½ tbsps. garam masala
- 1 tbsp. ground cumin
- 1 cinnamon stick
- 1 tsp. fenugreek seeds
- 2 tsps. ground turmeric
- Almonds for garnish (toasted, slivered)
- 1 tbsp. fine sea salt
- cilantro for garnish (freshly chopped)
- Garlic Naan for serving

Instructions

1. Pour a kettle of boiling water into a bowl containing cashews to soak for 30 minutes.
2. Meanwhile, heat 1/3 of the ghee in an Instant Pot with the "Sauté" function. Add the chicken, onion, and shallots. Sauté until the chicken turns brown and onion becomes translucent (for 8 minutes). Add in the remaining ghee with the bay leaves, cardamom, cinnamon stick, fenugreek, garam masala, garlic, ginger, lemon juice, tomato paste, tomato puree, salt, and turmeric and stir well to combine.
3. Tightly close the lid and select "meat/stew" on the pot or set to "Pressure Cook" and "Manual" and cook on "High" with the timer to 10.
4. In the meantime, drain the cashews and rinse very well. Pour the cashew inside an Instant blender with water up to ¾ full and blend on high speed until it is smooth and creamy. (This takes about a minute but about 30 seconds in a high-speed blender).

5. Once the timer beeps after cooking, do a quick pressure release and stir in the cream. Serve the butter chicken in serving bowls and sprinkle with almonds and cilantro and side with garlic naan.

Yield: 4 - 6 servings.

Jerk Chicken and Cornbread

Ingredients (for chicken and cornbread)

- oz. corn muffin mix (1 box to be prepared according to directions on the package)
- 2 tbsps. scallions (thinly sliced)
- 1 jalapeno (seeded and minced)
- 1 tbsp. olive oil
- 1/3 cup chicken broth
- 2 lbs. chicken thighs (boneless skinless)
- Lime wedges and additional scallions (sliced, optional for garnish optional)

Ingredients (for jerk mixture)

- 2 tbsps. Molasses
- 2 tbsps. lime juice
- 2 tbsps. Paprika
- 1 ½ tbsps. olive oil
- 1 ½ tbsps. garlic powder
- 1 ½ tsps. Allspice
- 1tsps. ground nutmeg
- ¼ tsp. pepper
- 1 tsp. kosher salt
- ¾ tsp. cayenne (or to taste)

Instructions

1. Stir in the scallions and jalapeno to the corn muffin mix prepared according to directions on the package. Coat silicone egg bite mold inside with nonstick spray and pour in the muffin batter.
2. Tap the counter to let the batter be even, release, and bubble and just cover the lid of the Instant Pot without sealing.
3. In a medium bowl, add jerk mixture ingredients and stir well to combine. Then, reserve half of the mixture and set aside. Then, add olive oil to the Instant Pot and sauté.
4. Have the remaining jerk mixture coat the chicken thighs and brown the chicken on both sides (each side for about minutes). Do this in batches so that you don't crowd the Instant Pot. Then, arrange the browned chicken in a shallow dish to be covered with foil.
5. Pour the broth into the pot and use a wooden spoon to scrape the brown bits from the pot to deglaze.
6. Arrange the chicken to the pot evenly in layers. Then spread the mixture on the chicken.
7. Lower the steam rack carrying the egg bite mold with a foil sling onto the riser.
8. Select "Cancel" to turn off the pot. Then, tightly close the lid and set the pot to "Manual" or "Pressure Cook" and set the timer to 10 minutes. Once the timer beeps after cooking, allow the natural pressure release for another 5 minutes and do a quick release of the remaining pressure.
9. Serve with cornbread. Garnish with additional sliced scallions and lime wedges.

Yield: 4 servings.

Honey Sesame Chicken

Ingredients

- 1 tbsp. olive oil
- 2 lbs. chicken thighs (boneless skinless)
- ½ cup onion (diced)
- 2 cloves garlic (minced)
- ½ cup soy sauce (low-sodium)
- ¼ tsp. red pepper flakes
- ¼ cup ketchup
- 1/3 cup honey
- 2 tsps. sesame oil (toasted)
- 2 tbsps. scallions thinly (sliced)
- 2 tbsps. cornstarch
- sesame seeds

Instructions

1. Pour olive oil to the Instant Pot and select "Sauté".
2. Add the chicken to the hot oil to brown on both sides (each side for about 3-4 minutes). Do this in batches so that you don't crowd the Instant Pot. Then, arrange the browned chicken in a shallow dish to be covered with foil. This time, it should not be cooked through.
3. Add onion to the pot, sauté for about 4 minutes to allow it to be soft. Then add garlic and continue cooking for 1 or 2 minutes more.
4. Add ketchup, red pepper flakes, and soy sauce to the pot, and then use a wooden spoon to scrape the brown bits from the pot to deglaze.
5. Re-add the chicken into the pot. Turn once to coat and turn off the pot.
6. Tightly close the lid and set the pot to "Manual" or "Pressure Cook" and set the timer to 5 minutes. Once the timer beeps after cooking, allow the natural pressure release for another 5 minutes and do a quick release of the remaining pressure.
7. Using tongs take the chicken out the pot and put on a cutting board. Then chop each into bite-sized pieces.
8. Add sesame oil and honey to the pot and stir well to combine.
9. In a small bowl mix together stir well the cornstarch and ¼ cup of pot liquid until thickened.
10. Add chicken back again to the pot and stir. Season to taste.
11. Serve hot over noodles or rice and garnish with sesame seeds and scallions.

Yield: 4 - 6 servings.

Chicken Marsala

Ingredients for dredge mix:

- 1/3 cup flour
- 1 ½ tsp. salt
- 1 tsp. pepper
- 1 tsp. garlic powder

Ingredients for Chicken Marsala:

- 2 lbs. chicken breast (thin-sliced)
- 2 tbsps. olive oil
- 2 tbsps. butter
- 1 shallot (finely diced)
- 3 cloves garlic (minced)
- 8 oz. mushrooms (sliced)
- ½ cup Marsala wine
- ½ cup chicken broth
- 2 tbsp. cornstarch
- 1/3 cup cream
- ¼ cup chopped parsley (optional, for garnish optional)

Instructions

1. Combine all dredge mix ingredients in a shallow bowl and coat chicken pieces in the dredge mix. Remove the excess by shaking off.
2. Add to the Instant Pot 1 tablespoon of olive oil and butter. Select "Sauté" and set to "High or More."
3. When the oil and butter melts, add the coated chicken pieces and brown until it turns golden, about 3 or 4 minutes per side. Do this in batches so that you don't crowd the Instant Pot. Then, arrange the browned chicken in a shallow dish to be covered with foil. This time, the chicken should not be cooked through.
4. Add remaining oil and butter with garlic and shallot the pot and sauté for about 3 minutes or until soft. Then add mushrooms continue cooking about 5 minutes more.
5. Pour wine and broth to the pot and use a wooden spoon to scrape the brown bits from the pot to deglaze. Add the back chicken to the pot and carefully arrange the meat in a single layer.
6. Select "Cancel" to turn off the pot. Tightly close the lid and set the pot to "Manual" or "Pressure Cook" and set the timer to 5 minutes. Once the timer

beeps after cooking, allow the natural pressure release for another 5 minutes and do a quick release of the remaining pressure.

7. Using kitchen tongs, transfer the chicken into a shallow dish arrange in a single layer. Then cover with foil.

8. Combine well ¼ cup of cooking liquid with 2 tablespoons of cornstarch in a small bowl. Then stir into the pot with the cream.

9. Cook and stir for about 5 minutes or until thickened. Start the "Sauté" function again as needed. Then, re-add chicken to the pot and cook for about 2 minutes.

10. Serve the chicken hot over mashed potatoes, pasta, or rice and garnish with parsley and fresh pepper.

Yield: 4 - 6 servings.

CHAPTER 8: TURKEY RECIPES

Turkey is a distinct poultry meal that also comes out great with or without best of seasonings, herbs, and spices. It lends itself to a lot of culinary versatility in special days. But you don't have to wait for the days of anniversary or Christmas parties before you enjoy your turkey if you have the Instant Pot. The following are various recipes.

Chinatown-Style Chop Suey With Ground Turkey

Ingredients

- ¾ cup of broth
- tbsps. soy sauce or tamari (regular or reduced-sodium)
- 3 tbsps. unseasoned rice vinegar (or 2 tbsps. apple cider vinegar)
- 1 tsp. ground dried ginger
- 1 lb. turkey (frozen, ground)
- 1 ½ lbs. or 6 cups of frozen unseasoned mixed vegetables (for stir-fry don't use any seasoning included)
- 2 tbsp. of water
- 1 ½ tbsps. of cornstarch
- Crunchy chow mein noodles (for garnish)

Instructions

- In the Instant Pot, mix well the chicken broth, ground ginger soy sauce or tamari, and vinegar. Position the pot rack (handles up) or an open large vegetable steamer in the pot. Arrange the block of ground turkey on the pot rack or vegetable steamer and tightly lock the lid.
- Set the pot on "Press Pressure" on "Max Pressure" and the timer to 17 minutes, ensuring that the "Keep Warm" function is off. Once the cooking is done, do a quick release to allow all pressure to escape and then unlatch the lid to open the cooker. Carefully remove the pot rack or vegetable steamer, allowing the block of turkey to fall inside the liquid.
- Using a meat fork and the edge of a large metal fork, break up the ground turkey into small pieces, rather than long threads. Arrange the vegetables on the meat top without stirring in the ingredients.
- Lock the lid back and set the pot to "Poultry," "Pressure Cook", or "Manual" and the timer to 10 minutes with the valve tightly closed.
- Once the time is up quick-release the pressure to bring the pressure back to normal and then and open the pot again.
- In a small bowl, whisk cornstarch and water until smooth.

- Select "Sauté" button and set to "Medium", "Normal," or "Custom 400°F" and the timer to 5 minutes. Allow it to simmer, while stirring often. Then stir in the cornstarch mixture and continue cooking. Keep stirring for about a minute until the liquid thickens. Then stop sautéing and use kitchen mitt or tongs to remove the insert from the pot. Set aside for a few minutes for it to thicken and stir well. Serve warm while sprinkling the chow mein noodles over the top.

Yield: 4 servings.

Cheesy Turkey Tacos

Ingredients

- 2 lbs. frozen turkey (ground)
- 2 cups or 16 oz. jar of chunky-style red salsa (mild or hot)
- ½ cup of turkey broth
- 4½ oz. or ½ cup of can chopped green chili (mild or hot)
- ½ cup frozen onion (chopped) or 1 small white or yellow onion (peeled and chopped)
- 2 tsps. standard chili powder
- ½ tsp. ground cinnamon
- 2 tsps. ground cumin
- 2 tbsps. yellow cornmeal
- Soft flour (for serving corn tortillas or taco shells can substitute)
- ¼ tsp. table salt (optional if the salsa is not rich in salt)
- Shredded lettuce (for serving)
- Shredded cheese (for serving)

Instructions

1. In an Instant Pot, combine well the salsa, broth, chili powder, cinnamon, cumin, green chili, onion, and salt (if using). Set the frozen turkey inside the pot for form an A-frame or a lean-to. Let them stick up out of the liquid and balance or lean against each other toward their upper edges.
2. Tightly close the lid select "Pressure Cook" on "Maximum Pressure" and set the timer for 20 minutes with the "Keep Warm" setting off. When done with the cooking, do a quick release of pressure to restore the pressure to normal and unlatch the lid to open the cooker. Using a meat fork and the edge of a large metal spoon, break the turkey into small bits.
3. Sauté by setting the pot to "Medium", "Normal", or "Custom 400°F" and the timer to 5 minutes.
4. Keep stirring almost constantly until the turkey mixture reaches simmer. Then stir in the cornmeal and allow it to simmer for about 3 minutes or until thickened. Stop sautéing and cover the pot without sealing and set aside to continue thickening for about 5 minutes.
5. Serve warm in tortillas with the lettuce and cheese.

Yield: 6 - 8 servings.

Turkey Breast and Mashed Potatoes

Ingredients

- 3 lbs. turkey breast (fresh, bone-in)
- 1 tbsp. oil
- ½ tsp. ground sage
- 1 tsp. dried basil (optional)
- 1 tsp. dried tarragon (optional)
- ½ tsp. thyme (or any other)
- 1 tsp. salt
- ½ tsp. pepper
- 1 ½ cups turkey broth or water
- 1 carrot (cut into 2 inches pieces)
- 1 stalk celery (cut into 2 inches pieces)
- 1 small onion (cut into 8 pieces)
- 2 to 4 russet of potatoes (peeled and quartered)

Ingredient (for gravy)

- ½. tbsps. butter (or oil)
- 2 tbsp. flour

Instructions

1. Wash the turkey breast and pat dry. Then rub a paste of oil, herbs, pepper, and salt all of over it.
2. Toss the vegetables (except the potatoes) into the Instant Pot inside the broth or water. Place the trivet over the mixture and arrange the turkey breast on the trivet. Add potatoes in a steamer basket that can fit inside the pot on or beside the turkey. (You can make a tin foil boat, if potatoes can't fit into the pot, to hold them and fit them elsewhere.)
3. Tightly close the pot ensuring that the valve is set to "Sealing." Then select "Pressure Cook" or "Manual" and set the time to 24 minutes.
4. When the pot beeps to indicate that the cooking is done, allow a 15-minute natural pressure release. (Meanwhile, if you want browned and crisped turkey skin, start the broiler and line your baking sheet with foil.)
5. When the pressure has completely released, press "Cancel" and flip the valve to "Venting" function to allow the pin to drop and open the Instant Pot. For browning, place your turkey breast on the baking sheet and fit it under the broiler to brown for no more than 5 minutes to avoid burning.
6. In the meantime, start mashing the potatoes while watching the browning turkey. Add the butter, pepper, and salt to taste.
7. To prepare the gravy, strain the liquid from the pot with a sieve and discard the vegetables.

8. Select "Sauté" and add butter or oil with the flour in the pot. Whisk for a minute unit the roux is cooked. Then add strained liquid at once and whisk very well.
9. Taste and if still needed, add pepper and salt. Then enjoy!

Yield: 4 servings.

Sweet Potato and Ground Turkey Chili

Ingredients
- 2 tbsp. extra-virgin olive oil
- 2 lbs. ground turkey
- 3 medium sweet potatoes (peeled, cut into 1-inch cubes)
- 1 medium red onion (or white, diced)
- 3 garlic cloves (minced)
- 4 celery stalks (chopped)
- 3 carrots (peeled and chopped)
- 1 red bell pepper (seeded and chopped)
- 14 ½ oz. tomatoes (diced) or 1 can
- 3 cups broth (low-sodium, could be chicken)
- ½ tsp. ground cumin
- ½ tsp. chili powder
- ¼ tsp. fine sea salt (optional)
- Fresh cilantro (chopped, for garnish optional)

Instructions
1. Pour the olive oil into the inner pot and sauté until it's hot. Add the ground turkey to the hot oil and continue sautéing for 2 minutes. Break up the turkey using a wooden spoon and be stirring to prevent it from sticking to the pot.
2. Stop sautéing to combine the sweet potatoes with the bell pepper, broth, carrots, celery, garlic, onion, and tomatoes inside the Instant Pot.
3. Tightly close the lid and choose "Pressure Cook or Manual" and cook on "High Pressure" while the timer is set 10 minutes. Check to see that the steam release knob is sealed. When it beeps after 10 minutes, allow natural pressure release for 10 minutes and then do a quick release of remaining pressure.
4. Open and stir in the chili powder, cumin, and salt (if using).
5. Serve garnished with fresh cilantro. It may be refrigerated in an airtight container for 4 days or freeze for 2 months.

Yield: 8 servings.

Turkey Pinto Beans Taco Salad

Ingredients

- 1 tbsp. olive oil
- 1 lb. ground turkey
- ½ tsp. salt
- ½ tsp. pepper
- 16 oz. fresh salsa (tub refrigerated)
- 15 oz. pinto beans (1 can, drained and rinsed)
- 2 tbsps. sour cream
- 1 head romaine lettuce (cut into pieces)
- 9 oz. tortilla chips (1 bag)
- 1 large avocado (to be diced)
- 1 cup (grated) cheddar or monterey jack cheese
- 6 oz. black olives (sliced)

Instructions

1. Sauté olive oil in the Instant Pot by selecting "Sauté" function on the display panel and set to "High or More." Pour the turkey into the hot oil and add pepper and salt. Continue sorting until the meat turns brown and no pink remains.
2. Add half the salsa and the pinto beans, stir well to combine then stop press "Cancel" to turn the pot off. Secure the lid and make sure that vent is closed. Then Select "Manual or Pressure Cook" on the display manual and set the timer for 4 minutes.
3. When the timer beeps, wait 4 minutes for natural pressure release and do a quick release of the remaining pressure.
4. Stir well sour cream and remaining salsa in a small bowl.
5. Serve with the proper portions of avocado, cheese, chips, lettuce, olives, and turkey and bean mixture in 4 bowls. Top with the salsa/sour cream dressing.

Yield: 4 servings.

Cornstarch Turkey Breast

Ingredients

- 7 lbs. bone-in turkey breast
- 3 tbsps. butter softened
- ½ tsp. paprika
- ¼ tsp. garlic powder
- 1 ½ cups broth (or water)
- 1 small onion (quartered)
- 2 small celery stalks (cut in half)
- 2 tbsps.+ 1 cornstarch
- ½ tsp. salt

Instructions

1. Thaw and clean the turkey breast of any gravy mix and giblets. Rinse and drain in a colander. Pat dry with paper towels and gently loosen the skin on the breast top with your hands and knife (but don't cut it off).
2. In a small bowl, add butter, seasoning, and salt. Use your fingertips to spread about 2 tablespoons of the mixture under opened the skin and extend it up to the breast. Cover the mixture back with the skin and spread the rest of the mixture on the outer part of the skin.
3. Position the trivet inside the Instant Pot and pour the broth. Place the celery and onion in the cavity if the turkey breast has and it is open. Then place the turkey in the Instant Pot with breast side up.
4. Tightly close the lid, ensuring that the valve is set to sealing. Select "Pressure Cook or Manual" and cook on "High Pressure" while the timer is set 32 minutes. It may take between 12 and 20 minutes before it comes to pressure. When it beeps after 32 minutes, allow natural pressure release for 20 minutes. Switch to "venting" if some pressure still remains after 20 minutes for the pressure to completely escape and the floating valve to drop.
5. Preheat broiler while you use tongs or any other safe utensil to remove the turkey and place it on a foil-lined baking sheet. Bring to broil for 3 to 5 minutes or until the skin turns golden brown. It should be about 3-5 inches from the broiler.
6. Pour 2 cups of turkey drippings into the Instant Pot and throw away the remaining liquid, if it remains. Add celery and onion.
7. Separately combine well the cornstarch and water in a custard dish and then add these to the turkey drippings. Start the Instant Pot "Sauté" function to cook the gravy. Keep stirring constantly for about 8 minutes or until it is slightly thick.
8. Serve and enjoy!

Yield: 6 - 8 servings.

Turkey and Green Beans Stuffing

Ingredients

- 2 lbs. turkey breast (uncooked)
- ¾ cup of broth
- 6 oz. stuffing mix (1 box)
- 10 ½ oz. cream of chicken soup (1 can)
- 8 oz. Greek yogurt (sour, cream plain, or mayonnaise)
- 2 cups green beans (frozen)
- 1 tsp. pepper
- 1 tsp. salt
- Cranberry sauce (to taste)

Instructions

1. Cut the turkey breast into 4 and limit each piece thickness to 1 inch. Then season with pepper and salt.
2. Pour the broth to the Instant Pot and arrange the turkey pieces in an even layer.
3. Tightly secure the lid, ensuring that the vent is closed. Select "Manual or Pressure Cook" on the display panel and set the program the timer to 7 minutes.
4. In the meantime, gently combine and fold cream of chicken soup and sour cream (or yogurt or mayonnaise) together stuffing mix in a medium bowl.
5. When the timer stops, do a quick release of pressure and examine the turkey to see if it is fully cooked. If not, add 2 tablespoons of water, secure the lead again and this time set it to cook manually or pressure cook for 2 minutes more minutes. Then do a quick release one more time.
6. Set frozen green beans evenly in layers on the turkey and avoid stirring. Again, tightly secure the lid and set to "Manual or Pressure Cook" with the timer on 4 minutes. When the timer beeps, quickly release the pressure.
7. Serve hot immediately with cranberry sauce as a side.

Yield: 2 servings.

Instant Pot Turkey Chili and Tomato Chickpeas

Ingredients

- 1 lb. ground turkey (85% lean)
- 4-5 oz. of water
- 15 oz. chickpeas (previously cooked in the Instant Pot or any white bean)
- 1 yellow bell pepper (diced, another yellow bell pepper can be added)
- 1 onion (diced)
- 2-3 cloves of garlic (peeled but not chopped)
- 1 ½ tsps. cumin
- 1/8 tsp. cayenne
- 20 oz. tomatoes with chili (2 cans)
- 11 oz. tomato juice (1 can)
- 12 oz. vegetable stock
- 2 ½ tbsps. chili powder

Instructions

1. Pour water with turkey and into Instant Pot. Tightly secure the lid, ensuring that the vent is closed. Select "Manual or Pressure Cook" on the display panel and set the program the timer to 5 minutes.
2. When the timer beeps, allow up to 10 minutes for natural pressure release. Then, quick-release the remaining pressure. Open the pot and break up the turkey.
3. Add the rest of the ingredients and select the "Manual" while setting the timer to 5 minutes. After cooking, wait for 10 minutes for natural pressure release and do a quick release if any pressure still remains. Open the lid and stir. Then serve!

Yield: 3 - 4 servings.

Turkey One Pot Meal

Ingredients

- 2 turkey quarters roughly 2.5 pounds
- 1 medium onion (diced)
- 3 garlic cloves (minced)
- 1 large carrot (chopped)
- 1 celery stalk (chopped)
- 1 cup turkey or chicken stock (low sodium)
- 2 tbsps. olive oil
- A dash sherry wine
- 2 bay leaves
- A pinch of dried rosemary
- A pinch of dried thyme
- pinch of dried sage
- 3 tbsps. cornstarch (mixed with 2 tbsps. cold water as a thickener)
- 4-5 Yukon gold potatoes (or Russet potatoes, halved, about 2 ½ Lb)
- 1 oz. Parmesan cheese (freshly grated)
- 1/3 cup milk (or cream)
- 1 - 2 tbsps. butter (unsalted)
- kosher salt (to taste)
- black pepper (to taste)

Instructions

1. Pat the turkey quarters dry with paper towels and season with enough amounts of black pepper and kosher salt. Then select "Sauté" option. Let it continue to sauté until it brings the message "hot".
2. Bring the turkey to brown in your Instant Pot or on a skillet. Add half of the olive oil and place the turkey in the Instant Pot. Allow each side to boil for about 5 minutes. Then set aside.
3. Pour half of the unsalted chicken stock into the Instant Pot to deglaze and scrub off the flavorful brown bits from the bottom using a wooden spoon. Then reserve the flavored liquid.
4. Add the other half of olive oil to the pot and add the onion. Sauté for about a minute and add garlic. Continue sautéing for another 30 seconds until fragrant. Add salt, black pepper, celery, and carrot. Sauté for 5-7 minutes until the vegetable is slightly brown.
5. Add bay leaves, a pinch of rosemary, sage, and thyme and mix thoroughly. Sauté for 1 minute more.
6. Add a dash of sherry wine to the pot. Use a wooden spoon to scrub the brown bits to deglaze. And add browned turkey quarters, any reserved liquid, and the rest of

unsalted chicken stock in the Instant Pot. Carefully position a steamer basket inside the pot and add the Yukon gold potatoes.

7. Tightly close lid and set to cook on "Manual" High Pressure timed for 18 to 20 minutes. When the time is up, allow 10 minutes of natural pressure release. After the 10 minutes, turn the knob to "Venting" to release the remaining pressure. Open the lid carefully.

8. Carefully remove the steamer basket, pour the potatoes into a mixing bowl and mash with a fork or masher. Then add butter, milk (or cream), and Parmesan cheese. Continue the mashing and mixing until desired smoothness.

9. In the meantime, remove and set aside the turkey quarters. Press "Sauté" function to heat the Instant Pot. Continue mashing the potatoes and season with black pepper and salt to taste. You may add more milk or cream for creamier potatoes.

10. Mix cornstarch with water and stir the into the turkey gravy gradually until desired thickness. Serve while drizzling with the turkey gravy and mashed potatoes.

Yield: 2 - 3 servings.

Cranberry Braised Turkey Wings

Ingredients

- 2 tbsps. butter
- 2 tbsps. oil
- 4 turkey wings (2 to 3 Lb)
- Salt and pepper to taste
- 1 cup dry cranberries (soaked in boiling water for 5 minutes or 1 ½ cups fresh or 1 cup of canned cranberries to be rinsed)
- 1 medium onion (roughly sliced)
- 1 cup walnuts (with shells)
- 1 cup orange juice (freshly squeezed, prepared juice with no sugar added)
- 1 bunch thyme (fresh)

Instructions

1. Melt the butter and combine with the swirled olive oil in a preheated pressure cooker set on high heat and uncovered with the lid.
2. Add pepper and salt to the turkey wings to taste and brown on both sides; ensuring that both sides of the skin are nicely colored.
3. Take the wings out briefly and add onion to the Instant Pot. Then add the wings with the nicely colored skin side pointing up. Add cranberries, walnuts, and some bundle of thyme. Also, pour the orange juice over the turkey.
4. Then tightly close the pressure cooker. Set it to "High Pressure" with the timer on 20 minutes.
5. When timer beeps, wait for natural pressure release for about 10 minutes. Do a quick release of the remaining pressure.
6. Use tongs to carefully remove thyme. Take the wings to a serving dish carefully so that they do not fall apart as they will still be tender. Slide the dish under the broiler for about 4 minutes or wait until the wings are caramelized enough.
7. Reduce the cooking liquid to half.
8. Serve the turkey wings with the rest of the liquid, cranberries, onions, and walnuts.

Yield: 6 - 8 servings.

Thanksgiving Turkey and Gravy

Ingredients
- 4 ½ to 5 lbs. bone-in turkey breast
- 4 tsps. poultry seasoning
- ¾ tsp. fine sea salt
- 1 cup chicken broth (low-sodium)
- 2 tbsps. unsalted butter (melted)
- 2 tbsps. flour (all-purpose)
- 2 tbsps. heavy cream (optional)

Instruction
1. Pat dry the turkey breast and mix with the poultry seasoning and salt. Rub roughly half of the mixture on the turkey skin and in the cavity under the breast. Keep the remainder.
2. Pour the broth into the inner insert of the Instant Pot and place a trivet inside. Set the turkey breast on the trivet with the skin side up.
3. Tightly lock the lid ensuring that the valve is turned to "Sealing." Set to "Pressure Cook or Manual" and cook on "High Pressure" with the timer set to 15 minutes. When the timer stops, allow the pressure to release naturally for 8 minutes and then do a quick release of the remaining pressure by turning the valve to "Venting." Unlatch and remove the lid.
4. Meanwhile, preheat the oven to 400°F while mixing in the butter and the remaining seasoning.
5. Pour the pressure-cooked turkey on a rack on a rimmed baking sheet with the skin side up. Smear the seasoned butter on the turkey skin and roast for 10 to 15 minutes. Let the skin brown and check that the inner temperature is at least 155°F.
6. To make the gravy, take the ½ cup of the cooking liquid. Also, have the trivet removed from the Instant Pot. Leave the remaining liquid in the pot. Sauté over "Medium" heat. Stir together the flour and the cooking liquid while the remaining liquid in the pot simmers. Stir in the flour mixture gradually and cook for 3 to 5 minutes to bring the gravy boil thick. You may add more cream to your desired thickness.
7. Remove the turkey from the oven and allow it to rest for 10 minutes. Then slice and serve.

Yield: 4 servings.

CHAPTER 9: DUCK AND GEESE RECIPES

How nice would it be if duck and geese would be as common as turkey as chicken! They are a nice game for hunters and they will give you anything. In any case, they are delicious meat. However, they can be tough and take a lot of time to cook. The Instant Pot is up to the task. It will break them down into a nice meal. Try out the following recipes and testify.

Easy Duck à l'Orange

Ingredients
- 4 duck thigh (quartered, bone-in)
- 1 tsp. salt
- ½ tsp. pepper
- 1 tbsp. vegetable oil
- 1 cup chicken broth
- 1 cup orange juice
- ½. cup sugar
- Zest from one orange
- 1 tbsp. Grand Marnier (optional)
- 2 tbsps. cornstarch (mixed with 2 tbsps. of water to have slurry thin orange slices for garnish)

Instructions
1. Trim excess skin from duck quarters (if any). Sprinkle all sides of the meat with pepper and salt.
2. Press the Sauté button on the Instant Pot to heat the inner pot and wait for the message "hot." Then add the vegetable oil, letting it coat the bottom. Set the duck pieces into the hot pot, skin side down, in a single layer. You may do this in batches if the meat pieces are too large. Heat each side of the meat for about 4 minutes to allow it to turn golden brown on both sides.
3. Remove the duck from the pot and deglaze the pot. Then pour the chicken broth into the pot. With a wooden spoon, scrape the bottom so that all the brown bits will be scraped up. Combine the sugar and orange juice with the broth and stir repeatedly to allow sugar to dissolve completely. This will take about 2 minutes. Add also the orange zest and stir very well. Now stop sautéing.
4. Return the duck pieces into the pot with the skin side up. Tightly close lid having the valve turned to "Sealing". Pressure cook on high and set the timer to 12 minutes. When the timer beeps, allow the pot to sit for 10 minutes to naturally

release the pressure. Then release the remaining pressure by turning the valve to "Venting." In the meantime, turn on the broiler.

5. Now, open the lid use tongs to transfer the meat pieces to a broiler pan. Set the pan under the broiler and broil for 8-10 minutes for the duck skin to turn crispy. Meanwhile, start the "Sauté" and start sautéing the Grand Marnier (if using), cornstarch, and the water slurry. Whisk all together to form a thick sauce. Select "Cancel" to stop sautéing.

6. Take the duck out of the oven and set in on a platter. Serve and garnish with thin slices of orange.

Yield: 4 servings.

Duck Ragu in the Instant Pot

Ingredients

- 2 Culver duck legs
- 2 star anise
- 2 cloves of garlic (lightly crushed)
- 2 stems of rosemary (fresh)
- 1 rib of celery
- 1 small red onion
- 2 tbsps. tomato puree
- 3 tbsps. marsala wine
- Pinch of pepper (to taste)
- Pinch of salt (to taste)

Instructions

1. Slash the duck leg's skin several times so that it can render out the fat.

2. Sauté the legs for 10 minutes in the Instant Pot. Keep turning from time to time to let the skin brown and yield enough fat. (You need as much as you can possibly get, so you may strain it into a sterile jar, using some cheesecloth, and store in the fridge for future uses.)

3. Stop sautéing by selecting "Cancel" and keep the excess fat as said above. Add the duck legs back into the pot and add garlic, star anise, and one rosemary stem. Then cover with cold water. Tightly cover the lid, setting the vent valve to "Sealing." Cook on "Manual" with the timer on 45 minutes.

4. Pour the celery and onion into the Instant food processor and blend to fine confetti or soffrito. (Another option is to finely mince them up by hand using a sharp knife). Chop the other stem of rosemary, allowing it to yield approximately 2 teaspoons. Set aside for now.

5. Once the timer beeps, do a quick pressure release. Then drain the legs and keep the garlic cloves. Squeeze their content into the rosemary and soffrito. You no longer need the remaining herbs and spices and water.

6. Meanwhile, bring a large pot of water to boil and add salt, then the fresh pasta. Reserve a 250 ml cup of the pasta water. At this time you may be removing the skin from the duck's legs and be flaking the meat, using two forks.

7. Start again the "Sauté" function on the pot. Add a teaspoon of duck fat (reserved earlier) back into the pot. Combine this with garlic, rosemary, soffritto. Sauté for 2-3 minutes and allow to soften and fragrant. Stir occasionally.

8. It is not time to introduce the tomato purée to the pot. Stir thoroughly. Then deglaze using the Marsala. Now add the duck.

9. Combine all of the ragu ingredients to form a sauce using as much as desired of the pasta water. Season very well with pepper and salt to taste. Add the cooked and drained pasta and stir well to have the ragu distributed over the pasta ribbons.

10. Serve with generous amounts of Parmesan cheese and black pepper in deep bowls.

Yield: 2 servings.

Instant Pot Duck Gravy

Ingredients

- ½ tsp. herbes de Provence
- ¼ tsp. black pepper (freshly ground)
- 4 duck legs
- 2 tbsps. ghee duck fat (or avocado oil, divided)
- 8 garlic cloves (peeled and smashed)
- 1 medium celery rib (diced)
- 1 large carrot (diced)
- 1 medium yellow onion (diced)
- 1 tbsp. tomato paste
- ½ cup bone broth (or chicken stock)
- 1 medium navel orange
- 2 tbsps. Italian parsley (coarsely chopped)
- 1 fresh thyme sprig
- 1 bay leaf (dried)
- 1 ½ tsp. of Kosher salt

Instructions

1. Add kosher salt and pepper in a small bowl while you pat dry the duck legs using a paper towel. Sprinkle the seasoning over the meat.
2. Pour 1 tablespoon cooking fat into the insert of the Instant Pot when hot and start sautéing. Add carrots, celery, onion, and ½ tablespoon of salt to the fat when once it melts. Keep stirring occasionally while sautéing until the vegetables become soft. That takes about 4 to 6 minutes.
3. Then toss in the garlic, add tomato paste, and stir while you continue cooking it for 30 minutes to allow it to fragrant. Now add the broth and scrape up the brown bits.
4. Slightly peel the zest off the orange using a vegetable peeler to do it in strips. Squeeze out the orange juice and pour it into the Instant Pot. Then toss in the zest together with bay leaf, parsley, and thyme. Combine well and cancel the sautéing.
5. Set the seasoned duck legs inside the Instant Pot in a single layer with the skin side up. Tightly lock the lid, ensuring that the valve is on "Sealing" and set the pot to "High Pressure" with the time at 45 minutes.
6. Once the cooking is done, allow 20 minutes of natural pressure release and do a quick release of pressure thereafter. Remove the now tender duck leg carefully to prevent it from falling apart. (You may allow it to cool and store it in the fridge in an airtight container for 3 days.)

7. After removing the bay leaf, orange zest, and thyme sprig, use a food processor to blend the remaining content into a purée to make gravy. Taste to see if the seasoning is appropriate or if you still need to add. If it yields excess gravy, the extra may be frozen for up to 3 months in ice cube molds.
8. You may now fry the duck legs over medium-high heat in the nonstick skillet using the remaining fat. Allow each side to fry for 3 minutes or until the skin becomes golden brown and crispy.
9. Then serve and enjoy with the gravy.

Yield: 2 servings.

INSTANT POT DUCK CONFIT

Ingredients

- ¾ tbsp. and 1 ½ tsps. kosher salt
- 4 tsp. ground black pepper (fresh coarse)
- 5 garlic cloves (peeled and smashed)
- cloves (lightly crushed with a rolling pin)
- 1 bay leaf (crumbled)
- 1 star anise
- ½ teaspoon allspice berry (lightly crushed with a rolling pin)
- 5 sprigs thyme
- 4 duck legs (about 8-12 oz. each)

Instructions

1. In a small bowl, combine allspice berries with bay leaf, cloves, garlic, pepper, and salt. Have the duck legs coated on all sides with the spice mixture and place them on a rimmed baking sheet. Refrigerate for a minimum of 24 hours and a maximum of 72 hours.
2. Then scrape the spices off the legs and reserve. Set the duck legs, skin side down in an Instant Pot and in an even layer and start the "Sauté" function on the pot. Sauté the legs for about 10 minutes for it to become golden brown.
3. Add ingredients to the pot and tightly close the lid, ensuring that the valve is set to "Sealing". Set the pressure to high and the time to 40 minutes and start cooking. When it beeps to indicate the end of cooking, do a manual quick release of pressure.
4. Take out the legs carefully and serve.
5. Alternatively, you may want to crisp the skin by cooking further over medium-low heat in a skillet. You can also preserve for a while in a heat-proof container or bowl together with the fat and refrigerate after it has cooled down.

Yield: 4 servings.

Braised Duck Breasts with Apples and Onions

Ingredients

- 2 tbsps. olive oil
- 4 duck breasts (about 1Lb each)
- **4 large** garlic cloves (to be thinly sliced)
- 2 large onions (½ lb., or 3 small onions to be sliced into ½ inches pieces)
- 4 medium Red Prince apples (½ lb. each, quartered and sliced into wedges with the core removed)
- 1 cup frozen cranberries
- ½ cup vermouth (optional)
- 2 cups stock (chicken or vegetable)
- 8-10 sprigs fresh thyme (more for serving)
- pepper (to taste)
- salt (to taste)

Instructions

1. Pat duck breasts dry with a paper towel at the room temperature. Then cut only the skin of the duck breast deeply and long in diagonal all the way through, using a sharp knife. Draw angles 90 degrees with the cuts to make diamond patterns. Season the duck breasts very well with salt and pepper.

2. Sauté the duck breast in the Instant Pot using one tablespoon of olive oil for about 6-8 minutes. Transfer the duck breast to a plate with the skin side up. Drain all the fat into a bowl and keep.

3. Return the breast into the Instant Pot and add about ½ tablespoon of the fat and onion. Cook on "High Pressure" for 5 minutes. When the timer beeps, do an instant release of the pressure.

4. Add olive oil into the inner inset, add garlic with the duck breast and cook for about 1 or 2 minutes. Deglaze the pan by adding the vermouth to and scrape out of the bottom all the onion and duck bits. Then allow the vermouth to evaporate.

5. If you want it fattier, you may add 1-2 tablespoons of the duck fat and then add, apple wedges and thyme leaves. Then season with pepper and salt to taste.

6. Stir well to allow apple-onion mixture to move around and create space for the duck breasts. Re-add the duck breasts to the pan, setting them skin side up between the mixture.

7. Then pour the stock to the pot, tightly cover with the lid and boil on medium pressure for 60 minutes.

8. When the timer beeps, allow the natural release of pressure for about 20 minutes and quick release the remaining pressure. When all the pressure is gone, remove the lid and cook a bit more on high for about 4 minutes to reduce the sauce.

9. Once the sauce is a bit reduced, add half of the frozen cranberries and mix with a spoon. Then transfer the meat to an oven-compliant pan to broil in the oven for about 3-5 minutes for the skin to get crispy and golden brown.

10. Serve with any of mashed potatoes, rice, steamed vegetables, quinoa, or even buckwheat.

Yield: 4 servings.

Goose in Red Wine and Prunes

Ingredients

- ¼ cup duck or goose fat (or vegetable oil / clarified butter)
- 1 medium onion (diced)
  1 cup of celery (diced)
- 3 carrots (peeled and roughly chopped)
- 1 tsp. salt
- 1 tsp. pepper
- 1 tsp. dried thyme
- 8-10 prunes (sliced in half)
- 1 cup red wine (full-bodied)
- 1 cup water (or chicken broth)
- 1 wild goose (5-6 lbs. skinned and quartered, 2 breasts, 2 leg quarters)

Instructions

1. Heat the duck fat in your Instant Pot set to medium heat. Add onion, carrots, and celery when hot and cook for about 3 minutes for the onion to become translucent. Add pepper, prunes, thyme, and salt and sauté for 1 minute.
2. Next, add the chicken broth and wine and simmer for about 3- 5 minutes. Keep stirring occasionally.
3. Set the goose parts into the pot with legs as the base and breasts on top. Tightly cover and use according to your cooker's instruction. Generally, you have to set it on high pressure and set the timer to 60 minutes. When the cooking stops after 60 minutes, allow the natural release of pressure and do a quick release of the remaining pressure and remove.
4. Serve with any main course.

Yield: 6 servings.

Buttered Hot Goose

Ingredients:

- ½ cup butter (or margarine, 1 stick)
- 1 cup carrots (shredded)
- 1 cup celery (diced)
- 1 cup onion (finely chopped)
- 1 medium apple (cored, peeled, and chopped)
- 4 garlic cloves (finely chopped)
- 1 cup chicken stock
- ½ cup white wine (dry)
- ¼ cup fresh parsley (chopped, or 2 tbsps. dried)
- 1 ½ tbsps. rosemary (dried)
- 1 ½ tbsps. thyme (dried)
- 4 bay leaves
- 1 tsp. salt
- 1 tsp. pepper (cracked)
- 1 cut up wild goose (up to 10 lbs.)

Instructions

1. Melt 2/3 of the butter in the Instant Pot over medium heat. Add the goose parts to the heated and melted butter and brown lightly. Do this in two batches for evenness and remove from the pot to a plate and set aside.
2. Add the reaming stick of butter to the cooker to heat and melt it. Add the onion with apple, carrots, celery, and garlic to the pot when the butter is hot and sauté for 10 minutes.
3. After sautéing, add the stock, together with bay leaves, parsley, rosemary, wine, thyme, pepper, and salt and stir well. Heat all to bring to boil for 1 minute and reduce the heat. Allow the mixture to simmer for about 7-8 minute over medium-low heat.
4. Now add goose parts back into the pot and sprinkle some of the liquid over it. Tightly close the lid and program the pot to high pressure with the time set for 60 minutes. After cooking, let the pressure release naturally. This takes about 10 - 15 minutes. Carefully remove the lid and serve with any side dishes like couscous or potatoes.

Yield: 6 servings

Sous Vide Duck Breast

Ingredients

- 2 halves of duck breast (boneless, skin-on)
- 8 cups of water
- 1 tsp. salt
- ½ tsp. black pepper
- 2 tsp. garlic (freshly minced)
- 1 tbsp. vegetable oil
- 1/3 tsp. thyme (dry)
- 1/3 tsp. peppercorn
- 1 tbsp. apricot (peeled, cored, mashed with 2 tbsps. water
- 2 tsps. sugar

Instructions

1. Thoroughly clean the duck breasts and smear all ingredients. Refrigerate for 2 hours to chill and have the ingredients absorbed.
2. After 2 hours, rinse off spices and seal the duck breasts up in a Ziploc bag after removing the air.
3. Pour the water into the Instant Pot. While the lid remains open, start the pot and select "Keep Warm" option for 20 minutes. Drop the Ziploc bag with its contents in a water bath for 40 minutes.
4. Then take the bag out of the water and pat dry the breasts. Sear the skin side of the meat in a nonstick skillet over medium-high heat, adding 1 tablespoon of vegetable oil and allow it to turn golden. Do that to the other side by turning it over for 20 seconds more.
5. Meanwhile, prepare your apricot sauce by mixing apricot with sugar in another small pot. Boil on medium-high heat and simmer at low heat after 4 minutes.
6. Slice the duck breasts, serve with the apricot sauce and enjoy!

Yield: 2 servings.

Pickled Carrot Soup With Bacon

Ingredients

- 2 lbs. carrots (optional, peeled, a couple of small heirloom carrots are okay, to be thinly sliced)
- 4 cups broth duck
- ½ yellow onion (finely chopped)
- ½ pack bacon (cut into ¼-inch pieces)
- Salt to taste
- 1-2 tbsps. maple syrup (or to taste)
- ½ cup apple cider vinegar (to be added gradually, after tasting, if needed)
- White vinegar (as needed)

Instructions

1. In a skillet, cook the bacon and onions together until bacon is cooked and yet soft, and onions become translucent.
2. Pour the thinly sliced carrot into a small cup or bowl. Cover them with enough white vinegar. They should remain until the soup is finished. Chop the other carrots into 1-inch long pieces and combine with the broth inside the Instant Pot.
3. Set the pot to "Manual/High" and time for 4 minutes. When timer beeps, allow natural pressure release.
4. Put the cooked carrots inside an Instant blender and break them down into a smooth soup.
5. Stir in bacon and onions together with apple cider vinegar, maple syrup, and salt to taste. (The apple cider should be gradual and not overpowering. Taste as you add in bits to see when it is already moderately vinegary.
6. Serve topped with pickled carrots and enjoy!

Yield: 6 servings.

CHAPTER 10: BEEF RECIPES

It can be safely said that beef is the most commonly consumed of all meats. The protein contents of its various parts will always bring it closer to human pots. And the animals from which it is derived are the commonest. It will be presumptuous of any cook or chef to claim to possess the knowledge of all the meals that beef can be processed into. With the Instant Pot, you can make just about anything of beef. Here are a few examples.

Melt-in-Your-Mouth Beef Gyros

Ingredients

- 1/3 cup beef broth
- 2 tbsps. olive oil
- 2 tbsps. lemon juice
- 1 tbsp. oregano leaves (dried)
- 2 tsps. garlic powder
- 1 ½ lbs. beef chuck (well-marbled, sliced into ¼- inch strips, roast across the grain) .
- 1 onion (sliced thin)
- ½ tsp. pepper
- 1 tsp. salt

Ingredients (for serving)

- Pita bread
- Lettuce
- Tomatoes (sliced)
- Prepared tzatziki sauce

Instructions

1. With exception of beef, add all other ingredients to the Instant Pot and stir to combine.
2. Then, stir in the beef and let it be coated with the ingredients.
3. Tightly secure the lid and check to ensure that the vent is closed.
4. Turn on the pot, programing it to "Manual or Pressure Cook" for 20 minutes.
5. When the timer beeps to indicate that cooking is done, allow the natural pressure release for 10 minutes. Then quickly release the remaining pressure.
6. Serve on pita and top with lettuce plus tomato and tzatziki sauce

Yield: 4 - 6 servings.

Texas Beef Brisket

Ingredients (for spice mixture)

- 3 tbsps. smoked paprika
- 3 tbsps. brown sugar
- 1 ½ tbsps. garlic powder
- 1 ½ tbsps. onion powder
- 1 ½ tsp. ground cumin
- 2 tsps. pepper
- 1 tsp. chipotle chili powder
- ¾ tsp. mustard (ground)
- 1 tsp. oregano leaves (dried)
- ½ tsp. cayenne pepper optional
- 2 tbsps. kosher salt

Ingredients (for Texas beef brisket)

- 4-5 lbs. beef brisket fat (trimmed to ¼ inch or less, cut into 2 pieces)
- ½ cup BBQ sauce
- 1 cup of water

Instructions

1. Combine all the spice mixture ingredients in a medium bowl and rub over trimmed brisket. Seal the brisket in a large ziplock bag (you may use another tightly-covered container) and refrigerate overnight or for, at least, 8 hours.
2. Insert the steam rack into the Instant Pot and add water. Arrange the pieces of brisket on the rack with the fat side up. Tightly secure the lid and check to ensure that the vent is closed.
3. Turn on the pot, programing it to "Manual or Pressure Cook" on the display panel while the time is set for 75 minutes.
4. When the timer beeps to indicate that cooking is done, allow the natural pressure release for 15 minutes. Then quickly release the remaining pressure.
5. Remove the meat carefully from the pot and put on a baking sheet covered with foil. Then brush in the BBQ sauce. Broil the brisket for about 5 minutes for it to be caramelized and bubbly.
6. Slice the meat and serve.

Yield: 8 - 10 servings.

Quick Party Meatball Appetizer

Ingredients

- 32 oz. cooked meatballs (frozen)
- 12 oz. grape jelly (raspberry or red currant can do)
- 1 ½ cups BBQ sauce
- Chives (optional, chopped, for garnish)
- 1 cup of water

Instructions

1. Pour the water into the Instant Pot and carefully put the steam rack.
2. Put the frozen on a steamer basket and gently lower the basket onto the steam rack in the pot.
3. Tightly secure the lid and check to ensure that the vent is closed.
4. Turn on the pot, programing it to "Manual or Pressure Cook" on the display panel while the time is set for 10 minutes.
5. When the timer beeps to indicate that cooking is done, allow the natural pressure release for 10 minutes. Then quickly release of the remaining pressure.
6. Gently remove the steamer basket and the steam rack carrying it from the pot. Throw away the cooking water.
7. Then select "Cancel" to turn the pot off and now turn on the "Sauté" on the display panel.
8. Add the BBQ sauce and grape jelly to the pot. Cook, stirring until both have melted and combined.
9. Then return meatballs to the Instant Pot and toss to coat with the mixture.
10. Serve warm. You may garnish with chives.

Yield: 8 servings.

Beefy Potato Au Gratin

Ingredients (for the spice mixture)

- 1 tbsp. Italian seasoning
- ¼ tsp. Rosemary (crushed)
- 2 tsps. paprika
- ¼ tsp. pepper
- 1 tsp. salt

Ingredients (for the beefy potato au gratin)

- 1 lb. ground beef (preferably 93% lean)
- ½ + ¾ cup beef (or chicken) broth
- 1 ½ cups cheddar (shredded)
- 2 ½.lbs. russet potatoes (cut into ¼.-inch slices)
- Parsley (optional, chopped fresh, for garnish)
- ¼ tsp. pepper
- 1 tsp. kosher salt

Instructions

1. Combine all the spice mixture ingredients in a small bowl.
2. Pour the ground beef to the Instant Pot and sauté to brown.
3. Continue sautéing, stirring repeatedly until all pinks are gone. Then get the browned meat to a dish and loosely cover with foil.
4. Cancel the sauté to turn off the pot and rinse with cold water. Then coat the pot with nonstick spray.
5. Add to the pot one after the other ½ cup of broth, 1/3 of sliced potatoes, 1/3 of ground beef, 1/3 of cheese, and 1/3 of the spice mixture.
6. Do this again to the beef, cheese, potatoes, and spice mixture two times.
7. Then add the remaining ¾ cup of broth on the top.
8. Tightly secure the lid and check to ensure that the vent is closed.
9. Turn on the pot, programing it to "Manual or Pressure Cook" on the display panel while the time is set for 10 minutes.
10. When the timer beeps to indicate that cooking is done, do a quick release of the pressure. And serve hot!

Yield: 4 - 6 servings.

Beef Tips and Gravy

Ingredients

- 1 lb. sirloin steak (well-marbled, cut into 1-inch pieces)
- 1 tbsp. olive oil
- 1 onion (finely diced)
- 1 cup red wine
- 16 oz. baby bella (or crimini mushrooms, sliced)
- 2 cups beef broth (to be warmed)
- 1 ½ lbs. potatoes (cut into 1-inch cubes)
- 2 tbsps. butter
- 3 tbsp. cornstarch
- 2 tbsps. sour cream
- 1 tbsp. Worcestershire sauce (or Kitchen Bouquet or Gravy master)
- Italian parsley (chopped, for garnish, optional)
- 1 tsp. salt

Instructions

1. Sauté the olive oil in the Instant Pot using the "Sauté" function.
2. Add meat and onions to the hot oil and allow all sides of the meat to brown for about 5 minutes.
3. Then pour the broth and wine to the pot. Use a wooden spoon to deglaze by scraping the brown bits from the pot bottom.
4. Stir in mushrooms. Lower the default or any fitting steam rack or riser into the pot to be on top of the mushrooms. Then position the potato cubes in a steamer basket and place it on the rack or riser.
5. Cancel the sauté to turn off the pot. Tightly secure the lid and check to ensure that the vent is closed.
6. Turn on the pot, programing it to "Manual or Pressure Cook" on the display panel while the time is set for 15 minutes. When the timer beeps to indicate that cooking is done, do a quick release of the pressure.
7. Then carefully transfer the potatoes into a bowl and add butter, salt, and sour cream to it. Mash until it blends to your desired consistency.
8. Take the steam rack or riser out. Then stir in the Worcestershire sauce.
9. Combine ½ cup of the remaining liquid and cornstarch in a small bowl and add it into the pot and stir until it is thickened. Sauté as much as needed and adjust seasonings to taste.
10. Serve with mushrooms over mashed potatoes. You may garnish with the chopped Italian parsley, if using.

Yield: 4 - 6 servings.

Meatball Minestrone Soup

Ingredients

- 1 lb. ground beef
- 1 ½ tbsps. golden flaxseed meal
- ¼ cup tomato sauce (no-sugar-added)
- 1 large egg
- 1/3 cup mozzarella cheese (shredded)
- 1 ½ tbsps. Italian seasoning blend (divided)
- 1 tbsp. olive oil
- 1 ½ tsp. of garlic powder (divided)
- ½ medium yellow onion (minced)
- 2 garlic cloves (minced)
- ¼ cup pancetta (diced)
- 1 cup yellow squash (sliced)
- 1 cup zucchini (sliced)
- ½ cup carrots (sliced)
- 4 cups beef broth
- 14 oz. tomatoes (1 can, diced)
- ½ tsp. ground black pepper
- 3 tbsp. Parmesan cheese (shredded)
- 1 ½ tsp. sea salt (fine grind, divided)

Instructions

1. Preheat the oven up to 400°F. While the oven is heating, spread aluminum foil on large baking. Combine the ground beef, egg, flaxseed meal, ½ teaspoon of garlic powder, ½ tablespoon of Italian seasoning, mozzarella, tomato sauce, and ½ teaspoon of sea salt in a large bowl. Mix the ingredients thoroughly with your hands.
2. To make the meatballs, shape heaped tablespoon of the ground beef mixture into a ball. Do this to all the mixture. You should have several meatballs. Transfer each ball to the baking sheet you have already lined with foil and place them in the oven to bake for 12 minutes. Then remove the meatballs from the oven and set aside.
3. Start the "Sauté" function on the pot and select "Normal." Add olive oil, garlic, onion, and pancetta into the hot pot to sauté. Stir repeatedly for about 2 minutes for the garlic to become fragrant and the onion to soften. Then add the carrots, yellow squash, and zucchini to the pot and keep sautéing for 3 more minutes.
4. Then add the beef broth, black pepper, diced tomatoes, remaining garlic powder, Italian seasoning, and sea salt to the pot. Keep stirring to combine. Add the meatballs.
5. Tightly close the lid and check to ensure flip the steam release handle is in the "Sealing" position. Then cook on manual or high pressure with the time set for 5 minutes. When the timer beeps to indicate that cooking is done, allow the natural release of pressure for 10 minutes and do a quick release of the remaining pressure.

6. Gently open the lid and stir the soup. Serve hot with remaining ½ tablespoon of the Parmesan on each plate.

Yield: 6 servings.

Savory Barbacoa Beef

Ingredients (for marinade mixture)
- 6 oz. beer (or water)
- 4 oz. green chiles (diced, 1 can)
- 1 small onion (finely diced)
- 4 cloves garlic
- 3 in chipotles adobo sauce (or to taste)
- ¼ cup lime juice
- 2 tbsps. apple cider vinegar
- 1 tbsp. cumin
- 2 tsps. dried oregano leaves
- 1 tsp. pepper
- ¼ tsp. ground cloves

Ingredients (for savory barbacoa beef)
- 1 tbsp. olive oil
- 3 lbs. beef chuck roast (to be cut into 1-inch thick)
- 3 bay leaves
- 1 tbsp. kosher salt (or to taste)

Ingredients (for serving)
- Tortillas
- Avocado (diced)
- Cilantro (chopped)
- Red onion (diced)
- Lime wedges

Instructions
1. Combine all of marinade mixture ingredients in a food processor and blend to complete smoothness.

2. Start sautéing the olive oil into the Instant Pot. Add the meat to the pot when oil gets hot to brown both sides. It takes about 3 or 4 for each side to brown, though it will not be cooked through this time.

3. Add marinade to the Instant Pot. Then use a wooden spoon to deglaze by scraping brown bits off the bottom of the pot. Then add bay leaves and toss everything to ensure the meat is coated in the marinade.

4. Stop sautéing by pressing "Cancel" to turn the pot off. Tightly secure the lid and check to ensure that the vent is closed.

5. Turn on the pot, programing it to "Manual or Pressure Cook" on the display panel while the time is set for 60 minutes. When the timer beeps to indicate that cooking

is done, allow the natural pressure release for 15 minutes. Then quickly release the remaining pressure.

6. Do away with bay leaves and carefully transfer the meat out of the pot onto a cutting board to shred.

7. Re-add the meat to the pot, salt and toss them to coat.

8. Serve shredded beef with burrito bowls, nachos, salads, or tacos, alongside lime wedges.

Yield: 6 - 8 servings.

Short Rib Osso Buco

Ingredients (for osso buco)
- 4 sprigs thyme (fresh)
- 2 sprigs Rosemary (fresh)
- ½ lb. thick-cut bacon (cut into lardons)
- 8 bone-in beef short ribs (patted dry with a paper towel)
- 2 tsps. kosher salt
- ½ tsp. ground black pepper
- 2 tbsps. unsalted butter
- 1 onion (diced into ¼- inch pieces)
- 2 medium carrots (diced into ¼- inch pieces)
- 1 celery stalk (diced into ¼-inch pieces)
- 3 garlic cloves (thinly sliced)
- 1 tsp. tomato paste
- 2/3 cup dry red wine
- ½. cup beef stock
- 14.5 oz. tomatoes (diced, 1 can, drained)

Ingredients (for gremolata)
- ¼ cup fresh parsley (finely chopped)
- ½ lemon zest (finely grated)
- 2 garlic cloves (minced)
- Pinch of kosher salt (to taste)

Instructions
1. Use twine to tie thyme and Rosemary together and set aside.
2. Start "Sauté" function on the Instant Pot. Add bacon when it is hot and keep sautéing until it turns crispy. Then take the bacon out of the Instant Pot and set aside.
3. Rub the ribs with pepper and salt and introduce the ribs to the pot in batches and have all sides seared. Each batch will take 5 to 7. Transferred each seared short ribs into a plate and set aside.
4. Turn off the Instant Pot for 3 minutes to cool a bit. Melt butter in the pot as it is cooling and stir in the onions, carrots, and celery. Then return the Instant Pot to the Sauté mode to cook the vegetable to soft. This takes 4-5 minutes. Then stir in the thinly sliced garlic and tomato paste.
5. Pour in wine. Then deglaze by scraping brown bits off the bottom of the pot. Stir in tomatoes and stock and nestle beef back. Add the bundle of Rosemary and thyme.
6. Tightly cover the lid and set to "High Pressure" and timer to 40 minutes. When it stops, release the pressure naturally and quick-release the remaining pressure.

7. Take the meat out of the pot and simmer the sauce on "Sauté" function for about 5-7 minutes to thicken up. Meanwhile, combine well the gremolata ingredients in a small bowl.
8. Now, serve short ribs with sauce on top and sprinkle with gremolata.

Yield: 4 servings.

Korean Beef Bowl

Ingredients

- 2 tbsp. cornstarch
- ½ cup of water
- 1 tbsp. extra-virgin olive oil
- 2 lbs. flank steak (sliced into ½- inch thick strips)
- 3 garlic cloves (minced)
- ½ cup beef broth (low-sodium)
- 1/3 cup soy sauce (reduced-sodium)
- ¼ cup white wine vinegar
- 2 tbsps. honey
- 2 tsps. Sriracha sauce
- ¼ tsp. ground ginger
- 1 medium cucumber (sliced)
- 2 red bell peppers (seeded and sliced)
- 4 scallions (sliced, white and light green parts only)

Instructions

1. Whisk the cornstarch and water together in a small bowl to make a slurry. Then set aside.
2. Set the Instant Pot on "Sauté" and pour the olive oil into the inner insert of the pot. Add the steak and garlic when the oil is hot and sauté for 3 minutes. Keep stirring occasionally to allow all sides of the beef to brown evenly.
3. Cancel the sautéing to add the broth. Then, use a wooden spoon to deglaze by scraping brown bits off the bottom of the pot. Now add ginger, honey, sriracha, soy sauce, and vinegar and stir well to combine.
4. Tightly close the lid and check to ensure flip the steam release handle is in the "Sealing" position. Then cook on manual or high pressure with the time set for 10 minutes. When the timer beeps to indicate that cooking is done, allow a natural release of pressure for 5 minutes and do a quick release of the remaining pressure.
5. Unlatch and open the lid. Start to sauté. Using a slotted spoon, serve the beef.

Yield: 6 servings.

French Dip Sandwiches

Ingredients

- 3 cups beef (or chicken broth)
- ½ cup chopped onion (frozen) or 1 small yellow (or white onion, to be peeled and chopped)
- 1 tbsp. thyme leaves (stemmed) or 1 ½ tsp. dried thyme
- 1 tsp. onion powder
- 1 tsp. garlic powder
- ½ tsp. table salt
- ½ tsp. ground black pepper
- 2 lbs. beef (frozen, shaved)
- butter (to taste, for the sandwiches)
- 1 French baguette (to be cut into 4- to 6-inch length; each to be sliced open lengthwise)

Instructions

1. In the Instant Pot, combine and the broth with onion, garlic powder, onion powder, pepper, salt, and thyme and stir well. Arrange the frozen block of meat purposefully in the liquid mixture. Tightly lock the lid, check to ensure that the vent is closed. The cook on "Maximum Pressure" for 8 minutes and the "Keep Warm" setting should be off.
2. Then quick-release the pressure. When the pressure has returned to normal, unlatch the lid and open the cover. Using the edge of a large metal spoon together with a meat fork, break the meat into strips and chips.
3. Using tongs, transfer the chips and strips of meat into the lightly buttered baguette slices to make sandwiches. The liquid from the cooker (the hot broth) should be used as the dip for sandwiches. While serving.

Yield: 4 - 6 servings.

All-American Pot Roast

Ingredients

- 1 ½ cups beef broth
- ½ cup chopped onion (frozen) or 1 small yellow or white onion (to be peeled and chopped)
- 1 tbsp. Worcestershire sauce
- 2 tsps. Garlic (peeled and minced)
- 1 beef chuck roast (frozen, boneless, 3 to 3 ½ lbs.)
- 1 tsp. mild paprika
- 1 tsp. onion powder
- 1 tsp. dried thyme
- ½ tsp. ground black pepper
- 2 lbs. peeled root vegetables (e.g. butternut. carrots, potatoes, rutabaga, sweet potatoes, turnips and so on, cut into 2-inch chunks, and seeded as necessary)

Instructions

Combine all of the broth, garlic, onion, and Worcestershire sauce in an Instant Pot. Set the rack of the pot rack (with the handles up) inside the pot (You can also use a large open vegetable steamer that can fit in.) Set the frozen chuck roast carefully on the rack (or in the steamer). Mix thoroughly onion powder, paprika, pepper, and thyme and sprinkle the top of the meat with the mixture.)

Tightly lock the lid, check to ensure that the vent is closed. Cook on Maximum Pressure for 80 minutes while the "Keep Warm" setting is set on off.

Quick-release the pressure and open the cooker by unlatching the lid. Take the rack (or vegetable steamer) out of the pot by using kitchen tongs, cooking mitts, or any thick hot pad. Tip the chuck roast into the sauce. Dress the top of everything with the root vegetables.

Close the pot back. Cook on "High Pressure or Manual" and set the time for 10 minutes with the "Keep Warm" set to off and valve closed.

When the cooking stops, wait for about 30 minutes for natural pressure release. Then, unlatch the lid to open the cooker again. Use a large slotted spoon or a metal spatula with a meat fork to transfer the roast to a cutting board nearby. Allow to cool for a few minutes. Slice the meat into chunks and serve with the vegetables and sauce from the pot.

Yield: 6 servings.

CHAPTER 11: PORK RECIPES

Fatty Pork! Yums! It may be more than you think. Barbecues, soups, stews, chops, fingers, pastas, tacos, carnitas, and a lot more, pork is always there. You will find pork and its fat gracing your Instant Pot. Is it braised, pulled or tenderloin, with salsa, garlic, or styled? Pork can be anything for you. Come along here and let's explore what the Instant Pot can do to your pork.

Mongolian-Style Pork Stew

Ingredients
- 2 ½ lbs. pork shoulder (1 frozen cut-up bone-in)
- 1 tbsp. fresh ginger (peeled and minced) or 1 tsp. ground dried ginger
- ¾. cup apple juice (unsweetened, or cider)
- 1 ½ tbsps. honey
- ¼ cup soy sauce (regular or reduced-sodium) or tamari
- 1 lb. vegetables (4 to 5 cups, frozen, unseasoned, mixed, preferably an Asian--style blend, without the seasoning packet)
- 1 ½ tbsps. cornstarch (optional)
- 2 tbsps. of water (optional)

Instructions
1. Combine juice or cider, ginger, honey, and soy sauce or tamari in an Instant Pot and stir well. Then set the frozen pork meat in blocks of inside the mixture. Tightly lock the lid onto the pot.
2. On Max Pressure Cooker, use "Pressure Cook" method, setting the timer for 35 minutes while the "Keep Warm" setting is off. If it is on All Pressure Cooker, set it on "Meat/Stew" or manually pressure cook on "High Pressure" with the time on 40 minutes while the "Keep Warm" setting is off.
3. When the timer beeps after cooking time, quickly release the pressure to have the pressure of cooker back to normal. Then open the pot by unlatching the lid.
4. Stir the pork well to break it into chunks if it has not already broken. Stir in the unseasoned vegetable. Again, cover the pot and lock the lid. Select the "Meat/Stew" or manually pressure cook on "High Pressure" with the time set for 1 minute and the "Keep Warm" setting off. You may bring the liquid to simmer while you stir occasionally.
5. In a small bowl or medium teacup, whisk the cornstarch together with water while the liquid is simmering in the pot. Pour in the slurry, start stirring constantly and continue cooking for about a minute until the sauce has thickened.

6. Cancel the "Sauté" to turn off the pot and set it aside for a few minutes. Then serve when the sauce has set up.

Yield: 4 servings.

Italian-Style Braised Pork Chops

Ingredients

- 1 cup chicken broth
- 4 boneless pork loin chops (frozen, center-cut, 6- 8 oz. each)
- 2 tsps. stemmed thyme leaves(or 1 tsp. dried thyme)
- 2 tbsps. balsamic vinegar
- ¼ tsp. grated fresh nutmeg (or 1/8 tsp. ground nutmeg)
- 4 cups bell pepper strips (frozen, 16 oz. bag)
- ¼ tsp. red pepper flakes
- ¼ tsp. table salt

Instructions

1. In an Instant Pot, combine the broth, nutmeg, red pepper flakes, thyme, vinegar, and salt and stir well. Add the pepper strips and mix well. Then arrange the pork chops in a way that they will be upright, with one side leaning against each other and the other side against the insert. Don't stack to allow the space in between for liquid mixture and pepper strips. Then, tightly lock the lid onto the pot.
2. On Max Pressure Cooker, use "Pressure Cook" method, setting the timer for 16 minutes while the "Keep Warm" setting is off. If it is on All Pressure Cooker, set it on "Meat/Stew" or manually pressure cook on "High Pressure" with the time on 20 minutes while the "Keep Warm" setting is off.
3. When the timer beeps after cooking time, quickly release the pressure to have the pressure of cooker back to normal. Then open the pot by unlatching the lid.
4. Serving in plates and top with peppers and some of the sauce.

Yield: 4 servings.

Root Beer Pulled Pork

Ingredients

- 1 lbs. or 3- 4 pieces bone-in pork shoulder roast (visible fat removed)
- 2 tbsps. vegetable oil
- ½ cup root beer (good quality, regular)
- 1 cup barbecue sauce of choice (divided)
- 1 tsp. salt

Instructions

1. Start the "Sauté" function on the Instant Pot and set to "Normal." Add the oil and allow it to heat for 1 or 2 minutes.
2. Add the roast cut into 2 large pieces to the pot and let it cook each side for about 3 minutes and allow it to brown. Press "Cancel."
3. Whisk together the half of the barbecue sauce, root beer, and salt and pour the mixture evenly over the roast.
4. Then, tightly lock the lid onto the pot.
5. Use "Pressure Cook" or "Manual" and cook on "High Pressure" setting the timer for 45 minutes. Allow 10 minutes of natural pressure release and then use the quick pressure release to allow the remaining pressure to escape.
6. Transfer the meat to a large cutting board where it will cool down a bit. But it should still be warm.
7. Start "High Sauté" function and let the juices simmer for about 10–12 minutes. Keep stirring frequently until it becomes thick and reduced. (You should still have a cup of sauce).
8. Add the remaining barbecue sauce into the cooker. After shredding the meat, toss back to the pot to be coated with the sauce.
9. Serve as a main dish or on buns. Enjoy!

Yield: 6-8 servings.

Buttery Ranch Pork Chops

Ingredients

- 1 ½ to 2 lbs. boneless pork chops (4 - 6 chops)
- 2 + 6 tbsps. butter
- ½ cup of water
- 1 oz. dry ranch seasoning (1 package)
- 6 cups arugula (or spinach, optional)

Instructions

1. Sauté 2 tablespoons of butter in the Instant Pot by selecting "Sauté" function on the display panel. Set it to "More or High."
2. Brown the pork on both sides inside the hot butter, about 3-4 minutes per side. It will not be cooked through this time. You may do this in batches to avoid crowding the pot. Transfer the browned meat into a dish and cover with foil.
3. Pour the water into the pot. Use a wooden spoon to deglaze by scraping the brown bits from the pot bottom.
4. Return the brown meat to the pot and top with the remaining butter. Then sprinkle ranch over the top.
5. Select "Cancel" on the Instant Pot to turn the pot off. Then tightly close the lid, ensuring that the vent is closed.
6. Use "Pressure Cook" or "Manual" and cook on "Low Pressure" setting the timer for 30 minutes. When the pot beeps showing the end of cook time, allow 5 minutes of natural pressure release and then use the quick pressure release to let out the remaining pressure.
7. Carefully transfer the meat to a serving plate, cover loosely with foil.
8. If using, add your arugula or spinach to the pot. Stir evenly until wilted.
9. Pork chop is ready to serve on a bed of greens with the drizzle of the remaining sauce.

Yield: 4 servings.

Shredded Pork Ragù Pasta

Ingredients
- 1 ½ - 2 lbs. boneless pork shoulder (or butt cut in half)
- 2 tbsps. olive oil
- 1 medium carrot (chopped)
- 1 onion (finely diced)
- 2 cloves garlic (minced)
- ½ cup beef broth
- 3 tbsps. tomato paste
- 1 tsp. dried oregano
- 1 tsp. dried thyme
- 14.5 oz. tomatoes (diced, 1 can undrained)
- 2 tbsps. cornstarch
- 12 oz. fettuccine (prepared according to directions on the package)
- ¼ tsp. pepper
- 1 tsp. kosher salt
- Parmesan (shredded, for garnish)

Instructions
1. Sauté the olive oil in the Instant Pot by selecting "Sauté" function on the display panel.
2. Add onion to the hot oil in the pot and sauté for 3 minutes. Then add carrot and sauté for 3 minutes more. Next to add is garlic and then tomato paste and continue sautéing for 2-3 minutes more.
3. Add broth and seasonings. Then use a wooden spoon to deglaze by scraping the brown bits from the pot bottom. Add tomatoes and stir. Add meat and turn it once to coat.
4. Select "Cancel" on the Instant Pot to turn the pot off. Then tightly close the lid, ensuring that the vent is closed.
5. Use "Pressure Cook" or "Manual" and cook on "High Pressure" setting the timer for 40 minutes. When the pot beeps showing the end of cook time, allow 15 minutes of natural pressure release and then use the quick pressure release to let out the remaining pressure.
6. Carefully transfer the meat to a cutting board to shred.
7. Mix together the cornstarch and ¼ cup of pot juices and cornstarch. Keep stirring in the pot until thickened.
8. Transfer the meat back to the pot. Then fold in the formed pasta.
9. Top with the parmesan while serving hot.

Yield: 4-6 servings.

Pork Tacos with Pineapple Salsa

Ingredients (for pork tacos)
- 1 ½ lbs. country ribs (or pork shoulder, to be cut into 2-inch strips)
- ½ tsp. dried oregano
- ¼ tsp. ground cumin
- Pinch cinnamon
- 1 tbsp. extra-virgin olive oil
- ¼ tsp. black pepper (freshly ground)
- 4 garlic cloves (pressed)
- 2 tbsps. Orange Juice (to be freshly squeezed)
- 4 or 6 small corn (or flour tortillas, warmed)
- ¼ cup lime juice (freshly squeezed)
- 1 tsp. kosher salt
- 1 tsp. liquid smoke (optional)

Ingredients (for the salsa)

- 4 oz. or ½ cup pineapple (fresh, trimmed, and chopped)
- ¼ small red bell pepper (seeded, chopped)
- ¼ small onion (chopped, into about 2 tbsps.)
- 1 small serrano pepper (or jalapeño, seeded and chopped)
- 2 tbsps. chopped cilantro
- 1 - 2 tsps. freshly squeezed lime juice
- ¼ tsp. kosher salt (to taste)

Instructions
1. Combine all of the cinnamon, cumin, olive oil, pepper, salt, liquid smoke (if using), and orange juice in a small bowl. Sprinkle the mixture over the country ribs. Rub the spices into the meat lightly. Leave the rib for at least 30 minutes or up to overnight, if refrigerated.
2. Add garlic and lime juice to the inner insert and arrange the ribs in the pot in a single layer. Then tightly close the lid ensuring that the vent is closed. Use "Pressure Cook" or "Manual" and cook on "High Pressure" setting the timer for 25 minutes.
3. Meanwhile, prepare the salsa by mixing the bell pepper, cilantro, lime juice (to taste), pineapple, and salt in a medium bowl.
4. When the pot beeps showing the end of cook time, allow 10 minutes of natural pressure release and then use the quick pressure release to let out the remaining pressure.
5. Open the pot by unlatching the lid and using tongs, transfer the ribs to a plate or cutting board. Shred the meat using forks or hands into bite-size chunks and discard any gristle or fat.
6. Serve, adding ¼ cup of pork with a tortilla with a spoonful of salsa as the topping.

Yield: 2 servings.

Pork Carnitas

Ingredients

- 2 tbsps. pork lard (Manteca, or vegetable oil)
- 2 ¼ lbs. pork shoulder (roast or Boston butt, cut into 2-inch pieces)
- 1 tsp. coarse salt
- 1 tsp. ground cumin
- ½ tsp. black pepper (freshly ground)
- 1 cup orange juice (freshly squeezed)
- ¼ cup lime juice (freshly squeezed)
- 2 bay leaves

Instructions

1. Sauté the Manteca in the Instant Pot by selecting "Sauté" function on the display panel on "More or High".
2. Add pork to the melted Manteca and fry until it turns golden brown. That takes about 6-8 minutes. Then season with cumin, pepper, and salt and add the lime orange juices. Top with bay leaves.
3. Then tightly close the lid, ensuring that the steam release valve is on "Seal." Use "Pressure Cook" or "Manual" and cook on "High Pressure" setting the timer for 25 minutes.
4. When the pot beeps showing the end of cook time, allow natural pressure release and remove the bay leaves.
5. Shred the pork carnitas using two forks.
6. Serve immediately.

Yield: 6-8 servings

Pork and Hominy Stew (Posole)

Ingredients
- 1 lb. pork shoulder (cut into bite-size cubes)
- 1 - 3 canned chipotle chili in adobo (chopped, plus 1 to 2 tsps. adobo sauce, from the can, about ½ of a small can)
- 1 yellow onion (chopped)
- 25 oz. hominy (1 can un-drained)
- 3 - 4 cloves garlic chopped
- 2 tsps. ancho chili powder (or more, if needed)
- 2 tsps. ground cumin
- 1 tsp. dried oregano
- ¾ cup of water
- 1 tsp. salt plus more if needed
- ¼ cup cilantro (fresh, for garnish)

Instructions
1. Combine all the ingredients, except ancho chili powder and cilantro, in the Instant Pot and mix thoroughly.
2. Then tightly close the lid on the pot, ensuring that the pressure release valve is on "Seal." Use "Pressure Cook" or "Manual" to cook on "High Pressure" and set the timer for 30 minutes.
3. When the pot beeps showing the end of cook time, leave the pot to go on natural pressure release.
4. Taste to see if the pork is done and the degree of seasoned. If needed, season with more chili powder and salt.
5. Serve by garnishing with the cilantro.

Yield: 8 servings.

Savory Mole Pork Tacos

Ingredients (for savory mole pork tacos)

- 2 cups salsa (fresh)
- 2 tbsps. chili powder
- 2 tbsps. oregano (dried)
- 2 tbsps. cocoa powder (unsweetened)
- 1 tbsp. kosher salt
- 2 ½ lbs. butt (or shoulder, boneless pork cut into 3 pieces)
- ¾ cup beef broth
- 1 onion (quartered)

Ingredients (for serving)

- Corn tortillas (warmed)
- Sour cream
- Cilantro (chopped)
- Additional salsa
- Lime wedges

Instructions

1. Combine all ingredients, except the beef broth and onion, in a medium bowl. Toss to coat.
2. Add the broth into the Instant Pot, followed by the onion.
3. Arrange pork pieces evenly in one layer on the onions.
4. Pour any remaining marinade on the pork without stirring.
5. Then tightly close the lid on the pot, ensuring that the pressure release valve is on "Seal."
6. Use "Pressure Cook" or "Manual" to cook on "High Pressure" and set the timer for 60 minutes.
7. After 60 minutes of cook time, allow 10 minutes of natural pressure release and then do a quick pressure of the remaining pressure
8. Carefully transfer the pork meat to a cutting board to shred.
9. Add the meat back into the pot and stir well to combine.
10. Serve the pork on tortillas with cilantro, sour cream, salsa, and lime wedges,

Yield: 6 servings.

Soy Ginger Pork and Rice

Ingredients (for rice mixture)
- 2 cups long grain white rice rinsed
- 2.5 cups Water

Ingredients for (meat mixture)
- 1 tbsp. oil (or bacon drippings)
- 1 ¼ lbs. boneless pork chops (1 - 1 ½- inches thick)

Ingredients for (sauce mixture)
- 1/3 cup soy sauce
- 1/3 cup stock (chicken or beef)
- ¼ cup brown sugar
- 2 tbsp. ginger (fresh, minced)
- 1 clove garlic (minced)
- 1 tbsp. sesame oil (toasted)

Ingredients (for finishing)
- 2 cups broccoli florets (optional)
- 1 tbsp. cornstarch
- 1 tbsp. water

Instructions
1. Combine all ingredients for rice mixture in a 1.5-quart casserole dish. Sauté the oil in the Instant Pot by selecting "Sauté" function on the display. Then add pork to the hot oil to brown both sides for 3 or 4 minutes each side. It will not be cook through this time. The meat will not be cooked through this time. You do this in batches to avoid crowding the pot. Then transfer browned pork to a dish and loosely cover with foil.
2. Add all of sauce mixture ingredients to the pot. Using a wooden spoon, deglaze by scraping the brown bits from the pot bottom. Then add the meat back and turn once to coat. Lower a trivet or riser into the pot and lower the casserole dish on the riser with a foil sling. Don't let the bottom of the casserole touch the pork mixture.
3. Select "Cancel" on the Instant Pot to turn the pot off. Then tightly close the lid, ensuring that the vent is closed.
4. Use the "Pressure Cook" or "Manual" and cook on "Low Pressure" setting the timer for 14 minutes. When the pot beeps showing the end of cook time, allow 10 minutes of natural pressure release and then use the quick pressure release to let out the remaining pressure.
5. Remove the casserole and trivet and quickly move pork to a cutting board to cool a bit.
6. If using, it's time to stir in the broccoli florets to combine. Set the pot to "Keep Warm" for 3-5 minutes while the lid is closed so that the broccoli can be almost

tender. In a small bowl, mix the cornstarch and with cold water and stir into the broccoli sauce to thicken on "Sauté" mode.

7. Slice the meat against the grain and serve with rice topped broccoli and sauce.

Yield: 4 - 6 servings.

Road Map: Barbecue Pork Loin

Ingredients
- 1 ½ cups purchased barbecue sauce (of any sort)
- 1 cup thin liquid (water, any sort of broth, any sort of beer, or unsweetened apple cider)
- 3 lbs. or 1 package pork loin (frozen, boneless, center cut)

Instructions
1. Combine the liquid and barbecue sauce in an Instant Pot. Arrange the pork loin carefully in the pot with the fat side down. Allow it to coat in the sauce by turning it once for the fat side to be up. Lock the lid onto the cooker.
2. On Max Pressure Cooker, use "Pressure Cook" method, setting the time to 45 minutes while the "Keep Warm" setting is off. If it's on All Pressure Cooker, set it on "Pressure Cook or Manual" and cook on "High Pressure" with the time on 50 minutes while the "Keep Warm" setting is off and the valve closed.
3. When the timer beeps after cooking time, do natural pressure release to have the pressure of the cooker back to normal. Then open the pot by unlatching the lid.
4. Check the internal temperature of the pork loin to be sure that it is 145°F or more. (There is an instant-read-meat thermometer for this purpose that you can insert into the center of one or two of them). It is not safe to eat if not. So let it go through another round of high pressure cooking with the time set for 10 minutes. This time, do a quick release.
5. Take the pork loin out of the pot to a cutting board and set aside for about 7-10 minutes.
6. Sauté on "Medium, Normal, or Custom 300°F" with the timer on 20 minutes.
7. Let the sauce simmer in the cooker while you stir occasionally until it reaches reduced consistency for a thick barbecue sauce. This takes some 12 minutes.
8. Cancel the "Sauté" to turn off the pot and set it aside for a few minutes.
9. Slice the pork into ½-inch-thick pieces and serve with the sauce as a topping.

Yield: 6 servings.

Barbecue Pork Chops

Ingredients

- Spice Mixture (you may substitute 3 tbsps. of favorite pork rub)
- 2 tsps. brown sugar
- 1 tbsp. paprika
- ½ tsps. chili powder
- ½ tsps. garlic powder
- ½ tsps. onion powder
- ¼ tsp. pepper
- ¼ tsps. cayenne (optional)
- 2 tsps. salt

Ingredients (for BBQ Pork Chops)

- 1 ½ cups chicken broth
- 2 tbsps. olive oil
- 4 bone-in pork chops
- 1/3 cup BBQ sauce

Instructions

1. Combine all the spice mixture ingredients in a small bowl and season pork chops on both sides with it.
2. Sauté olive oil in the Instant Pot by selecting "Sauté" function on the display.
3. Add the pork to the hot oil and allow it to brown on both sides, about 4 minutes per side. It will not be cooked through this time. You may do this in batches to avoid crowding the pot. Remove the browned pork meat and put in a shallow dish. Then, cover loosely with foil.
4. Add broth to the pot and use a wooden spoon to deglaze by scraping the brown bits from the pot bottom.
5. Return the meat into the pot.
6. Cancel the "Sauté" to turn off the pot and set it aside for a few minutes.
7. Then tightly close the lid, ensuring that the vent is closed.
8. Use the "Pressure Cook" or "Manual" and cook on "Low Pressure" setting the timer for 17 minutes. When the pot beeps showing the end of cook time, allow 10

minutes of natural pressure release and then use the quick pressure release to let out the remaining pressure.

9. Transfer the pork chops to a baking sheet lined with foil. Then smear with the BBQ sauce. Bring to broil until the pork is caramelized and bubbly (for about 3-4 minutes).

10. Serve immediately.

Yield: 4 servings.

Five-Spice Pork Ribs

Ingredients

- 3 lbs. baby back pork ribs
- 2 tsps. sambal oelek (Indonesian red chili paste) or Sriracha
- 1 tbsp. Chinese five-spice powder
- 2 tbsps. soy sauce
- 2 tbsp. fish sauce
- ½ cup Orange Juice (freshly squeezed from 1 large orange)
- 1 tsp. sugar
- 3 cloves garlic (minced)
- 1 tbsp. canola oil
- 2 shallots (diced)
- 2 inch-piece fresh ginger (peeled and minced)
- Pinch kosher salt

Instructions

1. Place ribs rib racks cut into slabs of about 3 ribs into a large small bowl and season lightly with salt.
2. Whisk together the five-spice powder, fish sauce, orange juice, sambal oelek, soy sauce, and sugar in a measuring cup or a small bowl. Set aside.
3. Sauté the oil in the Instant Pot by selecting "Sauté" function on the display. Then add the shallots into hot oil and stir occasionally 4 about 4 minutes to make it soft and slightly browned. Put garlic and ginger and cook for about 2 minutes or until fragrant. Next, add the juice mixture and allow it to simmer. Cancel the sautéing.
4. Add the five-spice sauce to the ribs and leave 5 minutes. Set the ribs in the pot on upright position and add the sauce over. Then tightly close the lid, ensuring that the valve to turned to "Sealing." Use the "Pressure Cook" and cook on "High Pressure" setting the timer for 25 minutes.
5. In the meantime, line a baking sheet with aluminum foil.
6. When the pot beeps showing the end of cook time, allow natural pressure release. Then carefully remove the lid and transfer the ribs to the baking sheet, using tongs. Then preheat the broiler.
7. Start sautéing again and allow the sauce simmer for 10-12 minutes until thickened. Smear the ribs, on the top side, with the sauce and broil for 4 minutes. Remove the baking sheet and ribs carefully from the broiler. Use tongs to turn the ribs over and rub the remaining sauce on them. Broil one more time for 3 minutes. And serve on a platter.

Yield: 6 servings.

CHAPTER 12: LAMB RECIPES

The lamp has not been given the regard it deserves in the community of meats. It is underrated and underused even though it can be a delicious meal any time, even though a tough one. The Instant Pot is designed to treat such meats to a sumptuous meal. It can be a formidable rival for any of beef, chicken, can pork. Here are some lamb recipes for your cooking delight.

Vortex Plus Pistachio-Crusted Lamb

Ingredients
- 1 rack of lamb (trimmed and Frenched, maximum of 7 inches in width and length)
- 1 tsp. fresh rosemary (finely chopped)
- 1/3 cup pistachios (finely chopped)
- 1 tbsp. butter (melted)
- 2 tbsps. panko breadcrumbs
- 2 tsps. fresh thyme (finely chopped)
- 1 tbsp. Dijon
- ¼ tsp. pepper
- 1 tsp. kosher salt

Instructions
1. Work the spit through the rack of lamb ribs on the meaty side just next to the bone. You may use a pointed metal skewer if you need to make a hole. Use the rotisserie forks to make a thread on each side and screws to firmly hold the rack in place. Season the rack with pepper and salt.
2. Position a drip pan at the bottom of the cooking chamber. Then select "Airfry" on the display panel and set the temperature to 380 °F and the timer for 12 minutes. The press "Start."
3. Wait for the display to show "Add Food." Then transfer the spit into the cooking chamber, using the rotisserie fetch tool. Secure the ends of the spit with the red rotisserie release lever. Close the door and select "Rotate."
4. Meanwhile, combine herbs, panko, and pistachios in a small bowl, drizzle on butter and toss to evenly distribute.
5. When the machine stops the "AirFry" program, take the rack out and smear the meaty side with the Dijon. Firmly press the pistachios mixture on all sides of the meat. Position the rack on a cooking tray with the meaty side up.
6. Press "Airfry" on the display panel again and set the temperature to 380 °F with the timer set for 7 minutes. Then press "Start."
7. Wait for the display to show "Add Food" then insert the cooking tray, let it be in the center. Ignore when the message "Turn Food" displays.

8. When the "AifFry" process stops, use the instant-read-meat thermometer to check if thickest part of the meat is up to 140 ° F hot. If not, cook for 3 minutes more and check again. Then take the rack out of the cooking chamber and allow it rest for 10 or more minutes.
9. Slice into individual chops and serve.

Yield: 2 - 3 servings.

Moroccan Lamb Tagine

Ingredients (dry)

- 2 tbsps. ginger (ground)
- 1 tbsp. cumin (ground)
- 1 tbsp. turmeric (ground)
- 1 tsp. allspice
- 1 tsp. cinnamon ground
- ½ tsp. cayenne pepper
- ½ tsp. sea salt
- 2 tbsps. brown sugar
- ¼ cup onion (dried)
- ¼ cup carrots (dried)
- ¼ cup celery (dried)
- ½ cup apricots (sliced, dried)
- ½ cup figs (sliced, dried)
- ½ cup almonds (toasted, slivered)

Ingredients (for cooking and serving)

- 2 tbsps. canola oil
- 2 lbs. lamb shoulder(boneless, cut into 1-inch cubes)
- Sea salt (to taste)
- Pepper (to taste)
- 4 cups broth (chicken or vegetable)

Instructions

1. In preparation, add all ingredients in jar one after in the listed order.
2. Start cooking by selecting the "Sauté" function to preheat the Instant Pot.
3. Once it shows hot on the display panel, add the oil which should thin immediately.
4. Meanwhile, use a paper towel to pat dry the lamb cubes and season well with pepper and salt and brown all sides for about 12 minutes.
5. Add other ingredients (jarred) to the Instant Pot and mix broth. Then stir well.
6. Tightly cover with the lid, ensuring that the vent is in "Sealed" position. Then "Pressure Cook" on "High Pressure" with the timer set for 15 minutes. When the cooking time is up, do the natural release of pressure for 10 minutes followed by a manual release of the remaining pressure.
7. Then serve in plates.

Yield: 6 - 8 servings.

Irish Lamb Stew

Ingredients

- 2 tbsps. olive oil
- 1 lb. lamb stew meat (cut into ¾-inch cubes)
- 1 onion (finely diced)
- 2 tbsps. flour
- 2 cups broth (chicken or beef, warmed)
- 1 lb. russet potatoes (peeled, cut into ½- inch dice)
- 2 carrots (cut into ½-inch dice)
- 8 oz. Guinness (or other dark beer)
- 1 ½ tbsps. tomato paste
- 2 tsps. salt
- 1 tsp. dijon
- 1 tsp. thyme (dried)
- 1 tsp. Rosemary (dried)
- ¼ tsp. pepper
- Flat-leaf parsley (for garnish, optional)
- Fresh ground pepper (for garnish, optional)

Instructions

1. Bring olive oil to boil by sautéing in the Instant Pot, starting the "Sauté" function on the display panel.
2. Put the meats into the hot oil and brown on both all side for 3 -5 minutes per side.
3. Continue sautéing as you add onion for another 3-4 until it becomes soft. Then sprinkle in flour and stir to coat the lamb.
4. Add the broth into the pot. Deglaze by scraping the brown bits off the bottom of the pot using a wooden spoon.
5. Then add the rest of the ingredients and stir well to combine.
6. Select "Cancel" to turn the pot off. Tightly secure the lid, ensuring that the vent valve is on "Sealing" and set to "Manual or Pressure Cook" function to cook for 15 minutes.
7. When the timer beeps to indicate the end of cooking, allow the natural pressure release for 10 minutes and quick-release the remaining pressure.

Yield: 4 - 6 servings.

Lamb and Rice Casserole (Lamb Dum Biryani)

Ingredients (for Rice and Lamb)
- 1 cup basmati rice
- ½ cup Greek yogurt
- ½ cup yellow onion (minced)
- ½ cup fresh cilantro (chopped)
- ¼ cup fresh mint (chopped)
- 1 Serrano chili (seeded, or mince if desired)
- 1 tbsp. fresh ginger (minced)
- 1 tbsp. garlic (minced)
- 2 tsps. garam masala
- 1 lb. lamb shoulder (or leg, trimmed and cut into cubes)
- ¼ tsp. cardamom (ground)
- ¼ tsp. cinnamon (ground)
- ¼ tsp. cayenne pepper
- 1 tsp. turmeric (ground)
- 1/8 tsp. cloves (ground)
- 1 tsp. salt
- 1 cup water

Ingredients (for garnish)
- 1 tsp. vegetable oil
- 1 yellow onion (thinly sliced)
- ½ cup cilantro (fresh)
- ¼ tsp. salt

Instructions
1. Rinse the rice in a colander under cool running water. Set aside to absorb some of the water.
2. In a large bowl, whisk to combine all ingredients for the lamb. Then, add the lamb and toss to coat. Let the mixture wait for 30 minutes at room temperature and set aside.
3. Meanwhile, to prepare the garnish, preheat the broiler to high, then line a baking sheet with foil.
4. Break the onion slices apart with fingers and arrange on the baking sheet. Season and drizzle with salt and oil. Broil the onions for 15 minutes, stir once or twice.
5. Cover the bottom of the Instant Pot with the lamb mixture and carefully spread the rice evenly all over the meat. Pour in the water carefully and gently push down on the rice to submerge in the water. (Don't mix.)

6. Tightly close the lid. Select the "Manual or Pressure Cook" program to cook for 6 minutes. Leave and allow the pressure to release naturally. Then serve topped with browned onion garnish and the cilantro.

Yield: 6 servings.

Ground Lamb Kheema

Ingredients

- 1 tbsp. ghee (or vegetable oil)
- 3 - 4 sticks Indian cinnamon (cassia bark) or ½ regular cinnamon stick (to be broken into small pieces)
- 4 cardamom pods
- 1 cup yellow onions (chopped)
- 1 tbsp. garlic (minced)
- 1 tbsp. fresh ginger (minced)
- 1 lb. lamb (ground)
- 1 tsp. garam masala
- ½ tsp. turmeric (ground)
- ½ tsp. coriander (ground)
- ½ tsp. cumin (ground)
- 1 cup frozen peas (to be thawed)
- ½ tsp. cayenne pepper
- 1 tsp. salt
- ¼ cup of water

Instructions

1. Heat ghee by starting the "Sauté" function on the Instant Pot. Once the ghee has melted, add cardamom pods and cinnamon sticks to the pot and allow them to sizzle for about 8- 10 seconds. Then add garlic, ginger, and onions. Stir constantly as it cooks for 2 to 3 minutes. Stir in the ground lamb and keep stirring for 1 to 2 minutes to break up the clumps. Add the cayenne, coriander, cumin, garam masala, salt, turmeric, and water.
2. Stop sautéing by selecting "Cancel." Then tightly lock the lid on the pot and ensure that the pressure-release is set to "Sealing." Pressure cook on "Manual" with the pot set to "High Pressure" and the timer for 10 minutes.
3. After the 10 minutes of cooking time, let the pot go through the natural pressure release for 10 minutes. Then allow a quick release of the remaining pressure. Add the peas and stir. Cover and leave for about 7 minutes for the peas to be heated through.

Yield: 4 servings.

Mediterranean Lamb Shanks

Ingredients (for marinade mixture)
- ¼ cup olive oil
- 3 cloves garlic (minced)
- 2 tbsps. brown sugar
- 1 tbsp. dried oregano (smoked paprika)
- ½ tsp. cumin
- 1 cinnamon stick
- kosher salt

Ingredients (for Mediterranean lamb shanks)
- ¼ cup olive oil
- 1 onion (chopped)
- 3 carrots (chopped)
- 2 bay leaves
- 2 cups red wine
- 4 cups beef broth (warmed)
- 3 tbsps. cornstarch
- 1 ½ - 2 lbs. lamb shanks (about 3 shanks, preferably skinless)
- 3 tbsps. cold water
- ¼ cup Italian parsley (chopped, for garnish, optional)

Instructions
1. Combine all ingredients for marinade mixture in a large bowl. Add the lamb shanks and allow to coat well, set aside as it continues to marinate for a minimum of 30 minutes.
2. After the 30 minutes, start sautéing ¼ cup of olive oil in the Instant Pot by selecting the "Sauté" function on the pot's display panel. Once the oil is hot, start browning all sides of the meat for 4 - 5 minutes per side. This time, the meat is not expected to be cooked through. You may have to do this in batches to avoid crowding the pot. Once the meat is browned, transfer to a shallow dish and loosely cover with foil.
3. Add bay leaves, carrots, and onion together with the remaining marinade in the pot and sauté for 3-4 minutes until onions become soft.
4. Add wine to the pot and use a wooden spoon to deglaze by scraping the brown bits from the pot's bottom. Then reduce and allow it to simmer for about 10 minutes. Add broth and the meat back into the pot. Turn it only once to coat.
5. Press "Cancel" to turn the pot off. Tightly lock the lid, ensuring that the pressure valve is on "Sealing." On the display panel, program the Instant Pot for "Manual or Pressure Cook" and set the timer for 30 minutes.
6. When it beeps to indicate the end of cooking time, allow a natural pressure release for about 18-20 minutes and set a quick release for the remaining pressure.
7. Then open the lid carefully and transfer the meat from the pot to a dish and loosely cover with foil and reserve the juices. Add the liquid only to the pot.
8. Mix cornstarch and cold water thoroughly in a small bowl. Add this to the pot and stir well until thickened. Start the "Sauté" function again as needed.

9. Serve lamb meat on noodles, mashed potatoes (white or sweet), or rice, topping it with gravy. Garnish also with chopped parsley.

Yield: 4 servings.

Sous Vide Rosemary Lamb Leg With Roasted Root Vegetables

Ingredients (for the lamb leg)

- 1-2 lbs. lamb legs
- ½ tsp. garlic powder
- 2 Rosemary sprigs (fresh)

Ingredients (for the roasted vegetables)

- 3 large carrots (peeled, coarsely chopped)
- 1 lb. fingerling potatoes (coarsely chopped)
- 1 sweet onion (diced)
- 2 parsnips (peeled and diced)
- 1 tbsp. Rosemary leaves (minced, fresh)
- 6 cloves garlic (coarsely chopped)
- 1 orange (to serve)

Instructions

1. To prepare the lamb leg, preheat a water bath to reach 130°F. Meanwhile, lightly add pepper, and salt to the lamb and then sprinkle with the garlic powder. Place the lamb leg in a sous vide bag with the Rosemary sprigs on top and seal. Put the bag in the heated water bath and allow it to cook for 3 to 4 hours until heated through. (It could be as long as 24 hours to be tenderized.)
2. To prepare the roasted vegetables, preheat an oven to reach 400°F. Meanwhile, add the olive oil to roasted vegetable ingredients and toss everything. Then add pepper and salt. Place on a baking sheet and cook in the oven until tender (about 30 to 60 minutes). Stir once or twice.
3. Bring the sous vide bag out of the water bath and remove the cooked lamb leg. Use a paper towel or sterile dishcloth to pat it dry thoroughly. Add small salt and quickly sear both sides for 1 or 2 minutes each or until slightly browned. Take it off the heat and cut the lamb into portions to serve. Add the roasted root vegetables to the plate and top with orange zest.

Yield: 4 servings.

Lamb and Chickpea Stew

Ingredients

- 1 cup dried chickpeas (to be soaked for 8 hours or overnight)
- 2 tbsps. vegetable oil (divided)
- 1 lb. lamb stew meat
- 1 large onion (chopped)
- 1 tbsp. garlic (minced)
- 1 ½ tsp. salt
- 1 ½ tsp. cumin (ground)
- 1 tsp. turmeric (ground)
- 1 tsp. coriander (ground)
- 1 tsp. cinnamon (ground)
- ¼ tsp. black pepper
- 1 ½ cups chicken broth
- 14 oz. tomatoes (diced, 1 can)
- ½ cup dried apricots (chopped, divided)
- ¼ cup Italian parsley (chopped, fresh)
- 2 tbsps. lemon juice
- 1 tbsp. honey
- Couscous (hot cooked)

Instructions

1. Rinse chickpeas thoroughly and drain. Heat 1 tablespoon of oil in Instant Pot by selecting "Sauté" function. Add lamb and cook for about 6 minutes for it to turn brown.
2. Add the other 1 tablespoon of oil and onion and cook for 3 minutes for it to soften, keep stirring. Add cumin, cinnamon, coriander, turmeric, pepper, and salt. Cook for 1 minute, stirring. Add broth and tomatoes and cook for two minutes, stirring. Deglaze by using a wooden spoon to scrape the browned bit from pot's bottom. Add chickpeas and apricots mix and stir well. Cook for 2 minutes.
3. Tightly close the lid and make sure that the pressure release valve is on "Sealing." Select "Manual or Pressure Cook" and set to 20 minutes of high pressure cooking.
4. When the timer beeps, do natural pressure release for 10 minutes, then allow a quick release of remaining pressure.
5. Sauté the rest of apricots for 5 minutes for the sauce to reduce and slightly thicken. Stir frequently, adding the honey, lemon juice, and parsley. Serve over couscous or any other grain meal.

Yield: 4 - 6 servings.

Lamb Korma

Ingredients

- 2 tbsps. amchur powder
- ½ tsp. ground cloves
- 1 tbsp. cumin (ground)
- ½ cup garlic (minced)
- 2 tbsps. ginger (minced)
- 1 cup plain yogurt
- 1 tbsp. black pepper (freshly ground)
- 1 tbsp. kosher salt
- 2 tsps. Kashmiri chili powder
- 1 ½ lbs. lamb stewing meat (cut into 2-inch pieces)
- 3 tbsps. vegetable oil
- 8 green cardamom pods (cracked)
- 3 cinnamon (2-inch pieces)
- 1 cup beef broth (low-sodium)
- ½ cup cilantro (chopped)
- ½ cup fried onions (store-bought, crispy)

Instructions

1. In a large bowl, whisk together the amchur, chili powder, cloves, cumin, garlic ginger, yogurt, pepper, and salt to form a yogurt mixture.
2. Add the meat to the mixture and stir well to have the meat evenly coated. Cover and store in a fridge for a minimum of 1 hour and a maximum of 8 hours.
3. Heat the oil for 1 minute in the Instant Pot set on the "Sauté" mode. Allow it to thin then add the cinnamon sticks and cardamom pods and cook for 1 minute for the fragrance to come out. Add the lamb and yogurt mixture. Stir in the broth and tightly close the lid on the pot. Check to be sure that the valve is on "Sealing" and then select "High Pressure" and cook for 25 minutes.
4. When the timer beeps to signal the end of cooking time, allow the natural pressure release for 10 minutes and then quick-release the rest of the pressure.
5. Add the cilantro and stir. Taste and check if more salt is needed. Then garnish the onions and serve.

Yield: 6 servings.

Lamb and Feta Meatballs With Tomato and Olive Sauce

Ingredients

- 1 ½ lbs. lamb (ground)
- 1 egg (beaten)
- ½ cup breadcrumbs
- ½ cup feta cheese (crumbled, add extra for garnish)
- 2 tbsps. parsley (finely chopped, add extra for garnish)
- 1 tbsp. mint (finely chopped)
- 1 tbsp. of water
- 4 garlic cloves (minced, divided)
- ½ tsp. kosher salt (add more for sauce)
- ¼ tsp. black pepper (add more for sauce)
- 2 tbsps. extra-virgin olive oil
- 1 onion (chopped)
- 1 green bell pepper (chopped)
- 28 oz. tomatoes (crushed with juice. 1 can)
- oz. tomato sauce (1 can)
- 1 tsp. oregano (dried)
- 1/3 cup Kalamata olives (pitted and chopped, optional)

Instructions

1. Combine the lamb with egg, breadcrumbs, feta, garlic, mint, parsley, pepper, and salt. Add water to form the mixture into 1-inch balls.
2. Start the Instant Pot on the "Sauté" mode to preheat the Instant Pot. Once the message "hot" shows on the display panel, add oil, onion, and bell pepper one after the other.
3. Cook for 2 minutes, stir in the remaining minced garlic and cook for 1 minute more.
4. Add the crushed oregano to with juiced tomatoes and tomato sauce. Then season with pepper and salt.
5. Carefully put the lamb meatballs and spoon the sauce over each ball.
6. Tightly lock the lid on the pot and select "Manual," set the timer 8 minutes and cook on "High Pressure." Do a quick pressure release when cooking is done.
7. Serve with the sauce and top with a sprinkle of feta cheese and parsley.

Yield: 6 - 8 servings.

Italian-Style Lamb Shanks with White Beans

Ingredients
- 2 2/3 tbsps. kosher salt (divided)
- 4 cups water
- 8 oz. cannellini beans (or white northern beans, dried)
- 4 lamb shanks (10 oz. each)
- 2 tbsps. extra-virgin olive oil
- ½ cup dry white wine (or dry white vermouth)
- 1 bay leaf
- 1 medium onion (quartered)
- 2 cloves garlic (minced)
- 2 large carrots (peeled, 1 quartered, 1 coarsely chopped)
- 1 small fennel bulb (optional, quartered, fronds reserved, optional)
- 2 cups chicken stock
- 1 medium tomato (seeded and chopped)
- Black pepper (freshly ground)

Instructions
1. Dissolve 1 tablespoon of water in a large bowl while the beans are soaked in the salty water for 8-24 hours at room temperature. Then rinse and drain.
2. Prep the lamb by sprinkling the shanks with 1 ½ teaspoon of salt. Cover the bowl with aluminum foil and leave for 20 minutes to 120 minutes at room temperature. If it has to stay longer, it has to be in the refrigerator.
3. Start the "Sauté" function to preheat the Instant Pot. Adjust to "More" to increase the heat and add oil to the hot pot until shimmers. Meanwhile, pat the lamb shanks dry with a sterile dishcloth or a paper towel and add 2 shanks to the pot. Cook and leave alone for 5 minutes until it browns. Repeat the process for the second side. Then to a plate and do the same to the remaining 2 shanks.
4. Add the wine and cook. Deglaze by using a wooden spoon to scrape any browned bits from the pot bottom. Simmer until the wine reduces to about half. Add the bay leaf, carrot, garlic, onion, and fennel (if using) to the pot. Transfer the shanks to the pot and add the stock.
5. Tightly close the lid into place and select "Manual" on the cooker, set the timer 35 minutes and cook on "High Pressure." When the pot is through with the cooking, wait 10 minutes for the natural pressure release. Then, allow a quick-release of remaining pressure. Carefully open and transfer the shanks to a plate.
6. Discard the vegetable after straining the sauce into a bowl (or better still, a fat separator). Allow the fat to rise for about 5 minutes. Then return the sauce into the pot. Remove as much as possible of the fat, using a spoon.

7. Add the beans with the carrot and tomato to the pot and be sure they are submerged in water by about 1 inch of liquid. (You may add stock now). Return the lamb shank also.
8. Tightly lock the lid on the pot. Select "Manual", set the timer for 10 minutes and cook on "High Pressure." After the 10 minutes of cooking, let the pressure release naturally for 10 minutes and then quickly release the remaining pressure before opening the lid.
9. Adjust the seasoning and add more if necessary. Sauté again on "Normal" and medium heat if you need to reduce the soup, adding more salt if necessary and seasoning with black pepper. Continue to simmer for the sauce thickens a bit more.
10. Serve the beans and a lamb shank as topping in a bowl. You may sprinkle with the fennel fronds (if using).

Yield: 4 servings.

Kheema Pav

Ingredients

- 1 tbsp. oil
- 1 tsp. cumin seeds
- ½ tsp. turmeric
- 1 tbsp. garlic (grated)
- 1 tbsp. ginger (grated)
- 1 large yellow onion (diced)
- 2 plum tomatoes (diced)
- 2 tsp. mild red chili powder
- 1 tsp. garam masala
- 1 tsp. salt
- 2 heaping tbsps. coriander powder
- 1 lb. ground lamb
- ½ cup cilantro (chopped, for garnish)

Ingredients (to serve)

- 1 tbsp. butter or ghee
- 8 potato rolls

Instructions

1. Start the Instant Pot on the "Sauté" mode to preheat the Instant Pot. Once the message "hot" shows on the display panel, add oil and cumin seeds. Toast for about 30 seconds and add turmeric powder, stir well to mix. Add garlic and ginger, mix well.
2. Add onion, sauté for a minute and cover for 2 minutes while cooking continues.
3. Combine tomatoes with red chili powder, coriander powder, garam masala, and salt. Mix thoroughly.
4. Add ground lamb and break it with a spatula. Add ½ cup of water (or 2 tablespoons if you want a thicker curry).
5. Close properly the Instant Pot, ensuring that the pressure valve is on "Sealing." Cook on "Manual/High" for 4 minutes and then do a natural pressure release.
6. Garnish with cilantro, serve hot with anything.

Yield: 4 servings.

Rack of Lamb

Ingredients

- 2 cloves garlic
- 1 - 1.25 lb. rack of lamb
- Salt (to taste)
- Pepper (to taste)
- 2 tsps. avocado or olive oil
- ¾ cup broth (beef or chicken)
- ¼ cup red wine (or additional broth)
- ¼ tsp. fresh rosemary (chopped)
- ¼ tsp. fresh thyme (chopped)
- 1 - 2 tbsps. cold butter (cut into 4 pieces of 1 inch each)

Instructions

1. Heat the Instant Pot by starting the "Sauté" function. Meanwhile, cut the garlic in half and season with pepper and salt. Then chop or slice the herbs and garlic cloves. Add the oil to the Instant Pot when the message "Hot" shows on the display panel. Then add the lamb turning the fat side down.
2. Let the meat brown and transfer the browned lamb into the plate. Cancel the sautéing and add the broth (and wine, if using) into the pot. Deglaze the pot by using a wooden spoon to scrape the brown bits off the bottom of the pot.
3. Add the chopped garlic and herb, and the lamb again. Put the ribs side down with the rib bones serving as a sort of trivet.
4. Secure the lid on the pot tightly and ensure that the valve is set to "Sealing." Select "Pressure Cook" or "Manual" and set the time to 1 minute.
5. When the cooker beeps that the time is up, allow 12 minutes of natural release of pressure. Shift the valve to "Venting" for the quick release of remaining pressure. Open the pot when the pin drops and transfer the lamb to a plate. Then cover loosely with a foil and allow it rest for about 8 minutes. Meanwhile, prepare the sauce.
6. Again start the "Sauté" function to boil the sauce until it reduces to about ½ cup. Add the cubes of butter one at a time and keep whisking vigorously to mix well. Season with more pepper and salt if needed.
7. Carve the lamb into chops. Drizzle with sauce as you serve in a plate.

Yield: 2 servings.

CHAPTER 13: SEAFOOD RECIPES

Preparing seafood is almost the simplest thing among the culinary activities. Different recipes, unlimited varieties of flavors, and quick cook time, plus versatility are among the reasons why seafood will always make an "A" list in kitchens. Cooking any seafood in an Instant Pot changes the complexion of the story entirely. This chapter highlights the best way to handle crabs, shrimps, fillets, cod, and a lot more seafood in your Instant Pot.

Shrimp and Avocado Salad

Ingredients

- 2 tbsps. coconut oil
- 1 lb. shrimp (thawed and deveined)
- 1 cup of water (filtered)
- 1 avocado (mashed)
- 1 cup bell peppers (chopped)
- ½ cup bok choy (a Chinese cabbage, chopped)
- ½ cup kale (chopped)
- ½ cup spinach (chopped)
- 2 tbsp. walnuts (chopped)
- ½ tsp. basil (dried)
- ½ tsp. black pepper (freshly ground)
- ½ tsp. ginger (finely grated)
- ½ tsp. parsley (dried)
- ½ tsp. turmeric (ground)

Instructions

1. Start the Instant Pot on the "Sauté" and add the coconut oil to the hot pot to allow it melt.
2. Pour in 1 cup of water and add the shrimp. Tightly close the lid having the pressure release valve on "Sealing" and select "Manual/Pressure Cook." With the time set to 3 minutes, cook on "Low Pressure."
3. Meanwhile, to make your salad, toss together the mashed avocado, bell peppers, bok choy, kale, spinach, and walnuts.
4. After 3 minutes, when the cooking has stopped, do a quick pressure release by carefully switching the pressure release valve to "Venting."
5. Unlatch to open the cooker, take out the shrimp and top with the tossed salad. Sprinkle evenly on top the basil, black pepper, ginger, parsley, and turmeric. Enjoy!

Yield: 4 servings.

Clam Chowder

Ingredients

- 2 cups coconut milk (full fat)
- 2 bay leaves
- ½ tsp. black pepper (freshly ground)
- 1 cup bone broth (grass-fed)
- 1 lb. cauliflower (chopped)
- 1 cup celery (finely chopped)
- 4 oz. small onion (thinly sliced, about ¼ onion)
- ½ tsp. (kosher salt)
- 7 oz. clams (chopped, 2 cans drained)
- 1 cup heavy whipping cream

Instructions

1. Pour the coconut oil inside the Instant Pot and bay leaves, black pepper, bone broth, cauliflower, celery, onion, and salt. Mix thoroughly.
2. Tightly close the lid, while move the pressure release valve to "Sealing" and select "Manual/Pressure Cook." With the time set to 5 minutes, cook on "High Pressure."
3. After 5 minutes when the cooking has stopped, wait for about 3 minutes to allow the pressure to naturally disperse and then do a quick pressure release by carefully switching the pressure release valve to "Venting."
4. Carefully open the cooker by unlatching the lid and use tongs to remove bay leaves. Then add the clams and whipping cream, stirring as you do.
5. Start the "Sauté" mode and allow it to cook for 3 to 4 minutes (or more if desired). Then serve.

Yield: 5 - 6 servings.

Crab Bisque

Ingredients

- 4 tbsps. butter (grass-fed, softened)
- 3 cups bone broth (grass-fed)
- ¼ cup bell peppers (chopped)
- ½ tsp. black pepper (freshly ground)
- ½ tsp. cayenne pepper (ground)
- 2 stalks celery (chopped)
- 8 oz. cream cheese (full-fat, softened)
- 1 lb. frozen crab meat (to be thawed)
- 1 tsp. old bay seasoning
- 4 oz. onion (thinly sliced, ¼ small)
- ½ tsp. kosher salt
- 14 oz. tomatoes (1 can, sugar-free or low-sugar, crushed)
- ¼ cup heavy whipping cream

Instructions

1. Gently melt the butter in the Instant Pot by setting it to "Sauté".
2. Pour in the bone broth, and then mix in all other ingredients.
3. Tightly close the lid, having the pressure release valve on "Sealing" and select "Manual/Pressure Cook." With the time set to 3 minutes, cook on "Low Pressure."
4. After 3 minutes when the cooking has stopped, do a quick pressure release by carefully switching the pressure release valve to "Venting." You can blend briefly in an immersion blender if you want a smoother soup.
5. Take the bisque out and serve.

Yield: 4 servings.

Spicy Garlic Salmon and Asparagus

Ingredients

- 2/3 lb. salmon fillet (patted dry, cut into 2 equal pieces of approx. 1-inch thick)
- 1 ½ tbsps. garlic (minced)
- 2/3 lbs. asparagus (cut thick pieces, in half lengthwise)
- 2 tbsps. butter (cut into pieces)
- 2 tsps. honey
- 1 small lemon (sliced thin)
- ½ tsp. red pepper flakes
- 1 cup of water
- Pepper (to taste, freshly ground)
- Salt (to taste)

Instructions

1. Add minced garlic to salmon fillets to coat.
2. Top half of the asparagus with one piece of salmon and arrange them on a large piece of foil. Drizzle with a teaspoon of honey on half of the lemon slices and red pepper flakes. Dot all round with half of the butter.
3. Close the foil to let it form a pouch and crimp its edges to seal.
4. Do the same to the other fillets.
5. Add water into the Instant Pot, insert the steam rack and carefully lower the foil pouch packets on to the steam rack.
6. Tightly close the lead by ensuring that the vent valve is on "Sealing". Start the "Steam" function on the Instant Pot and program it for 4 minutes (or 3 minutes if the salmon fillets are thin).
7. Do a quick release of the pressure after three minutes when the cooking has stopped. Gently remove the packets. Season with ground pepper and (salt to taste) and serve.

Yield: 2 servings.

Vortex Plus Salt-and-Vinegar Crispy Fish

Ingredients
- ½ cup flour
- ½ tsp. paprika
- 1 egg (beaten)
- ¼ cup mayonnaise
- 1 lb. cod fillets (or haddock or Pollack)
- 4 oz. salt and vinegar potato chips
- Lemon wedges (optional, for serving)
- Tartar sauce (optional, for serving)

Instructions
1. Place the potato chips in a ziplock bag crush, using a rolling pin or mallet, to the desired consistency (it could be like that of panko bread crumbs).
2. To make a set up for dredging; in a shallow dish, add paprika to the flour and combine the mayonnaise and beaten egg in another shallow dish. In yet another dish, add the crushed potato chips.
3. Cut the fish into 6 pieces and dredge each piece in each of the 3 mixtures starting with flour mixture, to the egg mixture, and then in the potato chip mixture. Press the crumbs firmly on both sides.
4. Then, divide the fish onto different cooking trays with space between each piece of fish. Remember to have the drip pan placed in the cooking chamber bottom. Now start "Airfry" mode from the display panel programming the temperature to 370 degrees while the time is set to 10 minutes on the display panel.
5. When the message "Add Food" displays, insert the cooking trays, on in the top-most and the other in the bottom-most position.
6. When the message "Turn Food" is displayed, switch the position of the cooking trays as such that the tray on the first tray goes to the last position and vice-versa. You may leave the fillets not flip the fillet.
7. At the end of the "AirFry program," remove the fillets from the cooking chamber and serve hot. Top with lemon wedges and tartar sauce (if serving).

Yield: 3 - 4 servings.

Cod Fillets with Tomatoes and Zucchini

Ingredients

- 28 oz. tomatoes (diced, packed in juice 3 ½ cups)
- ½ cup chopped (onion, frozen) or 1 small yellow or white onion (peeled, chopped)
- 4 oz. pimientos (diced, 1 jar, not to be drained)
- 1 tbsp. dried Provençal (or Mediterranean seasoning blend)
- 10 oz. zucchini (frozen, sliced); or 1 medium zucchini (2 cups, sliced into ¼-inch-thick rounds)
- 4 skinless cod fillets (frozen, 6 oz. each)

Instructions

1. Combine the tomatoes, onion, pimientos zucchini, and seasoning blend in an Instant Pot and stir well and tightly close the lid onto the cooker.
2. If cooking on the Max Pressure Cooker, select "Pressure Cook on Max Pressure" with the timer set for 3 minutes while the "Keep Warm" setting if off. But if cooking on All Pressure Cookers, select Pressure Cook or Manual" on High Pressure with the timer set for 4 minutes, "Keep Warm" setting off, and vent valve closed.
3. After the cooking time ends, do a quick release of pressure to have the pot's pressure returned to normal. Unlatch the lid to open the cooker cover. Nestle the fillets into the sauce and return the cover and tightly lock it onto the pot.
4. If you are cooking on Max Pressure Cooker, cook for 5 minutes on "Maximum Pressure" while the "Keep Warm" setting is off. On All Pressure Cooker, "Pressure Cook" or cook on "Manual/ High Pressure" for 6 minutes while "Keep Warm" setting is off and the valve is on "Sealed".
5. At the end of the respective cook time, use the quick pressure release method to bring the pressure back to normal. Then open the cooker by unlatching the lid.
6. Transfer the fish and sauce into bowls using a large spoon.

Yield: 4 servings.

Butter-Poached Mahi-Mahi

Ingredients

- 4 mahi-mahi fillets (frozen skinless, 6 ounces each, 5-6-inch-long)
- ½ tsp. ground black pepper
- 8 tbsp. butter (1 stick)
- ½ tsp. onion powder
- ½ tsp. mild paprika
- ½ tsp. table salt
- 1 ½ cups of water

Instructions

1. In a small bowl, combine the paprika with onion powder, salt, and pepper until it blends well.
2. Pour water into the Instant Pot and have the rack with handles up (or another pressure cooker-safe trivet) set inside the pot.
3. Set a 7-inch round baking dish that is pressure cooker compatible inside the cooker.
4. Then stack the fillets in the dish. Sprinkle each fillet with spice mixture to evenly coat. (½ teaspoon is okay on each fillet.)
5. You may cook on Max Pressure Cooker for 7 minutes, keeping the "Keep Warm" setting off. You may also cook on All Pressure Cooker on "Manual/High Pressure" for 8 minutes, keeping the "Keep Warm" setting off.
6. When the cooking time elapses, do a natural pressure release by bringing the pot's pressure back to normal. Open the cooker by unlatching the lid. Using thick hot pads, or silicone cooking mitts, take the baking dish out. Then using a metal spatula, transfer the fillets into plates one at a time. Add the buttery mixture in the baking dish.

Yield: 4 servings.

Low Country Boil

Ingredients

- 12 oz. beer (or the same amount of water, if not using beer)
- ½ cup of water
- 1 tbsp. garlic (minced)
- 3 ears corn (shucked and cut into thirds)
- 1 ½ lbs. red potatoes (egg-sized)
- 12-16 oz. kielbasa smoked sausage (1 package, cut into 2-inch pieces)
- 1 tbsp. cajun (optional, or creole seasoning)
- 2 tbsps. Old Bay seasoning, divided
- 1 ¼ lbs. shrimp (medium to large)
- 1 tbsp. lemon juice
- 1/3 cup butter (melted)
- ½ tsp. garlic powder
- Additional Old Bay (optional, for garnish)
- Cajun seasoning (optional, for garnish)

Instructions

1. Combine and stir well beer, garlic, and water in the Instant Pot.
2. Add to the pot corn, red potatoes, and kielbasa sausage and garnish with the cajun seasoning (if using). Also, top with 1 tablespoon of the Old Bay.
3. Secure the lid tightly, ensuring that making sure the vent is closed.
4. Set on "Manual / Pressure Cook" mode from the pot's display panel and use the +/- buttons to program the cooking to 4 minutes.
5. When the timer beeps to indicate the end of cooking time, quick-release the pressure.
6. Add shrimp and remaining 1 tablespoon of Old Bay with a sprinkle lemon juice over the top. Cover the lid back pot, and have the pot set the pot to "Warm" for 5 minutes for the residual heat to cook the shrimp.
7. Transfer the corn, potatoes, and sausage with shrimps to a platter using a slotted spoon.
8. Mix butter and garlic powder and pour the mixture on the over the shrimp. You may also serve as dipping on the side.
9. Garnish with cajun seasoning or/ and additional Old Bay and serve warm.

Yield: 6 servings.

Thai Seafood Curry

Ingredients

- 2 tbsps. oil (to be chosen from coconut oil, peanut oil, or any favorite neutral-flavored oil like avocado, canola, corn, grape, safflower, and vegetable)
- 1 ½ cups allium aromatics (chopped)
- ¼ cup fresh ginger (peeled, minced)
- 2 tbsps. wet curry paste (to be chosen from green, red, or yellow Thai curry paste; massaman or Penang curry paste can be also be used)
- 14 oz. tomatoes (diced, 1 can)
- 1 cup regular (or low-fat coconut milk)
- 1 ½ tbsps. fresh lime juice
- 1 ½ tbsps. light brown sugar
- 1 ½ tbsps. fish sauce
- 1 ½ lbs. fish or shellfish
- 1 lb. chopped quick-cooking vegetables

Instructions

1. Start "Sauté" mode to heat the pot for 10 minutes and add oil in the hot quart cooker for about 1 or 2 minutes. Add the allium and cook for about 3-4 minutes, keep stirring often until it is softened. Add ginger and cook for a few seconds when it starts producing aroma.
2. Add the curry paste and stir well to coat everything. Then add one after the other tomatoes, lime, coconut milk, fish sauce, and brown sugar. Stir well and allow the brown sugar to dissolve. Stop the "Sauté" mode to turn off the pot.
3. If you are using the Max Pressure Cooker, select "Pressure Cook on Max" while you set the timer for 5 minutes and the "Keep Warm" setting turned off.
4. If you are using All Pressure Cooker, select "Meat/Stew" and "Pressure Cook/Manual" with the time set for 7 minutes and "Keep Warm" setting turned off.
5. After the cooking time, bring the pressure of the pot back to normal by using the quick-release method.
6. Then open the pot by unlatching the lid.
7. Start the "Sauté" mode for 5 minutes.
8. Allow it get to the full simmer and then stir in the fish or shellfish with the quick-cooking vegetables. Let the sautéing continue while you stir gently for 4-5 minutes to allow the fish to cook through.
9. Then turn off the pot by canceling the "Sauté" function. Take the hot inset out and serve seafood curry warm.

Yield: 4-6 servings.

Fish Taco Bowls

Ingredients

- 4 cups cabbage (shredded)
- 2 tsps. chili powder
- 1 lime (halved, juiced)
- ¼ cup mayo
- 2 tbsps. pickled jalapenos (chopped)
- 2 tbsps. sour cream
- 3 tilapia fillets (4 oz.)
- 1 tsp. cumin
- 1 tsp. garlic powder
- 1 tsp. salt
- 2 tbsps. coconut oil
- 1 avocado (diced)
- 4 tbsps. cilantro (fresh, chopped)

Instructions

1. Combine cabbage, jalapenos, lime juice, and mayo, with sour cream in a large bowl and cover. Refrigerate for 30 minutes or more before serving.
2. Start the "Sauté" function on the Instant Pot. While the pot is getting hot, pat fillets dry with a paper towel and evenly sprinkle with seasonings. Add coconut oil to the hot pot and allow it to melt completely. Add tilapia pan and sear each side for 3 -5 minutes to cook fully. Once the fish can flake easily, Press "Cancel" to stop sautéing.
3. Cut the fish into bite-sized pieces and separate slaw into different bowls. Add fish on top.
4. Divide avocado in half and remove the pit. Then scoop out the flesh. Divide avocado among four bowls. Squeeze the other half of lime juice on each dish. Sprinkle with cilantro and serve.

Yield: 4 servings.

Mediterranean Fish Stew

Ingredients

- 2 tsps. olive oil
- 1 clove garlic (minced)
- ½ cup onion (chopped)
- ½ green bell pepper (cut into 2-inch pieces)
- ½ red bell pepper (cut into 2-inch pieces)
- ½ tsp. smoked paprika
- ½ potato (halved)
- 1 cup chicken broth
- 4 oz. cod fillet (1 cod fillet not frozen, or thawed if frozen)
- 14.5 oz. tomatoes (diced, 1 can)
- ¼ cup small cooked shrimp (thawed)
- 1 lemon wedge
- 1 tbsp. fresh dill (chopped)
- ¼ cup parsley (fresh, chopped)

Instructions

1. Turn the Instant Pot on by pressing "Sauté" and setting it on the "Normal" program. Add olive oil once the pot is hot.
2. Add the garlic and onions to the melted oil and cook. Keep stirring for 3 minutes, or until the onion and garlic begin to soften. Add the smoked paprika, red and green peppers, potato, tomatoes, and chicken broth.
3. Tightly close the lid and seal the vent. Set the program to "Stew" with the temperature on "Normal" and set to cook for 5 minutes.
4. Use a quick-release method when the time is up to allow the pressure out.
5. Carefully open the lid to add the cod fillet and close the lid back, seal the vent again and return to "Stew" mode but with the temperature at "Less" this time. Set to cook for 8 minutes.
6. Once the cooking time is up, again, use a quick-release method to allow the pressure to escape.
7. Gently open the lid to stir in the shrimp and close the lid back for 5 minutes, let the just added shrimp heat through.
8. Ladle fish the stew into a medium or large bowl and garnish with herbs with lemon wedge.

Yield: 1 serving.

Fish and Pineapple Tostadas

Ingredients

- 1 tbsp. vegetable oil (approx.)
- 20 oz. pineapple chunks (with juice, 1 can)
- ½ tsp. hot pepper flakes
- 1 ½ lbs. tilapia fillets (skinless, cut into large pieces)
- 8 Corn tortillas (6-inch)
- ¾ cup of water
- 1 cup deli-packed coleslaw
- 1 avocado (optional, cut into chunks)
- Salt (to taste)

Instructions

1. Turn on the Instant Pot on by starting the "Sauté" mode on Normal. When the message "Hot" displays, add 1 teaspoon oil and allow it to coat the pot at the bottom. Heat the oil until shimmering.
2. Add 1 corn tortilla and cook for 2 minutes, turn it once. When it is lightly brown, put in a plate and season with salt. If the plate is lined with a paper towel, it will drain quicker. Then, transfer drained corn tortilla to a foil sheet and repeat the same process with the remaining tortillas. Add more oil as and when necessary between tortillas. Wrap all the drained tortillas in foil to keep them warm.
3. Stop sautéing and turn the pot off by pressing "Cancel."
4. Set aside 2 tablespoons of pineapple juice and add to the pot the remaining juice. Add hot pepper flakes with water and stir. Then arrange tilapia but do not stir.
5. Cover and tightly lock the lid with the steam valve set to "Sealing." Program the pot to cook on
   "Low Pressure" for 3 minutes.
6. When the cooking is done, select "Cancel" and turn the release valve to "Venting." When the pin drops down, open the lid. Check to see if the fish is opaque and can flake easily when forked. If not, you may repeat the cooing process for 1 more minute.
7. Add the reserved 2 tablespoons of pineapple juice into coleslaw in the meantime.
8. Start serving tortillas, 2 layers on each plate, mostly overlapped. Spoon fish and pineapple on each tortilla and top with coleslaw. If using, garnish with chunks of avocado.

Yield: 4 servings.

Mango BBQ Fish Tacos

Ingredients (for fish mixture)

- 1 lb. catfish (or either of tilapia or flounder, to be cut into chunks)
- 1 tsp. garlic powder
- 1 tsp. paprika
- 1 tsp. kosher salt
- ¼ tsp. pepper

Ingredients (for sauce mixture)

- 1 cup fresh mango cubes
- ½ cup BBQ sauce
- 1-2 tsps. hot sauce
- 2 tbsps. olive oil

Ingredients for (coleslaw mixture)

- 1 ½ tsps. lemon juice
- 1 tsp. mayonnaise
- ½ tsp. sugar
- 1 tsp. vinegar
- Salt (to taste)
- ½ cup shredded cabbage

Ingredients (for serving)

- Corn tortillas (warmed)
- Additional fresh mango cubes
- Cilantro (chopped) and fresh jalapeno (optional, sliced)

Instructions

1. Combine all the fish mixture ingredients in a medium bowl and allow them marinate for 15 minutes.
2. Meanwhile, combine the sauce mixture ingredients in a food processor and thoroughly blend. Set aside.
3. Select "Sauté" function on the Instant Pot's display panel. When warm, add olive oil.

4. Add pieces of fish in a single layer to the hot oil and allow to cook for 3 minutes or until browned. Flip and repeat with the second side.

5. Add prepared mango sauce to the fish and turn the pot off by canceling sautéing. Then lock the lid tightly, ensuring that the vent is closed.

6. Cook on "Manual or Pressure Cook" function with the timer set for 5 minutes.

7. Meanwhile, whisk together all coleslaw mixture ingredients in a medium bowl except the cabbage. Then add cabbage, stir to coat.

8. When the timer beeps, allow the pressure to naturally release for 3 minutes and then do the quick release of the remaining pressure.

9. Serve the fish mixture over warmed tortillas to be topped with coleslaw and mango (and cilantro or jalapeno if using).

Yield: 4-6 servings.

CHAPTER 14: PASTA AND SIDE DISHES

Foods made from the flour are always parts of cuisines the world over. That is why hardly will a day pass that pasta will not be a meal in your neighborhood. However, you can add some more value to your pasta dishes if you take them through the Instant Pot.

Also, the enjoyment of a meal is not yet full if there are no sides to it. The list of side recipes is almost endless. You can form virtually all foods into a side dish. Here in this chapter, you will see the descriptions of 7 pasta and 7 side dishes recipes.

PASTA RECIPES

Weeknight Mac and Cheese

Ingredients

- 16 oz. elbow macaroni (uncooked)
- 2 tbsps. butter
- 4 cups of water
- 2 tsps. salt
- 12 oz. milk (evaporated, 1 can)
- 8 oz. sharp Cheddar cheese (grated)
- ¼ cup Parmesan cheese (grated)

Instructions

1. Combine all of the macaroni, butter, water, and salt in an Instant Pot.
2. Tightly lock the lid on the pot and set the vent valve to "Sealing." Then select "Pressure Cook" on "High Pressure" with the timer set for 4 minutes. Do a quick pressure release.
3. Then open and stir in the milk into macaroni followed by both cheeses. Stir well until they melt and combine well.
4. Serve warm.

Yield: 4 - 6 servings.

Tomato Sauce With Artichokes and Olives

Ingredients

- 2/3 cup olive oil (extra virgin)
- 3 cloves garlic (minced)
- 1 medium onion (diced)
- 32 oz. artichoke hearts (2 cans of 16 oz. each, drained and cut in half)
- ¼ cup fresh basil (washed and chopped)
- ½ cup Pitted kalamata olives (whole)
- 46 oz. crushed tomatoes (2 cans of 28 oz. each)
- ½ tbsp. oregano (dried)
- 2 tbsps. tomato paste
- ½ tsp. pepper
- ½ tsp. salt

Instructions

1. Press "Sauté" on the Instant Pot display panel and add olive oil.
2. Wait one minute to allow it to heat up.
3. Add the garlic and onion and sauté for one minute. Keep stirring often.
4. Add the artichokes, basil, and olives. Also, sauté for another minute. Keep stirring often.
5. Add the crushed tomatoes, oregano, tomato paste, pepper, and salt and keep stirring.
6. Tightly lock the lid on the Instant pot with the valve set on "Sealing." Choose the "Manual or Pressure Cook" setting and set the timer for 10 minutes on sealing.
7. Once the timer beeps at the end of cooking time, quickly release the pressure.
8. Serve hot and enjoy!

Yield: 4 - 8 servings.

Pasta Puttanesca

Ingredients

- 32 oz. jar pasta sauce (1 can)
- 3 garlic cloves (minced)
- 3 cups of water
- 1 tbsp. capers
- 4 cups pasta (dried, such as rigatoni or penne)
- ¼ tsp. red pepper flakes (crushed)
- 2 tsps. lemon zest (grated)
- ½ cup kalamata olives (pitted, sliced)
- ¼ tsp. black pepper (ground)
- 1 tsp. fine sea salt

Instructions

1. Add all other ingredients to the pasta in the insert of the Instant Pot and stir so that the pasta is coated.
2. Tightly lock the lid into place with the valve turned to "Sealing."
3. Select "Manual or Pressure Cook" and set the pressure to "High" and the time to 5 minutes.
4. When the timer counts down to zero, do a quick pressure release by carefully turning the valve to "Venting."
5. Once the pressure returns to normal, unlatch and remove the lid.
6. Serve warm and enjoy.

Yield: 6 servings.

Spaghetti Bolognese

Ingredients

- 1 tbsp. olive oil
- 1 lb. extra-lean ground beef (at least, 90% lean)
- 2 cups yellow onions (chopped)
- 1 cup celery (chopped)
- 1 cup carrots (peeled, chopped)
- 1 can Muir Glen tomatoes (organic, fire-roasted, crushed, undrained, 28 oz).-
  2 cups Progresso beef broth (from 32-oz. carton)
- 12 oz. uncooked spaghetti (broken in half)
- ½ tsp. salt

Instructions

1. Start the "Sauté" mode on the Instant Pot on normal.
2. Add the oil and allow to heat. Then add beef, onions, and salt to the oil and cook 8 to 10 minutes. Stir occasionally. When it is thoroughly cooked, stir in carrots and celery. Stop the sauté by selecting "Cancel".
3. Stir in the broth into the beef mixture.
4. Arrange spaghetti evenly over the mixture followed by tomatoes. Tightly secure the lid, setting the steam valve to "Sealing." Select "Manual" and cook on "High Pressure" with the timer set for 7 minutes. When the cooking stops, do a quick-release of pressure by setting the pressure valve to "Venting."
5. Immediately use the tongs to lift the spaghetti. It will be stuck together, but stir the mixture for about 1 - 2 minutes for the pasta to be completely separated.
6. Serve and enjoy.

Yield: 6 servings.

Homemade Hamburger Helper

Ingredients (for pot)

- 1 lb. lean beef (ground, preferably 93% lean)
- 1 tbsp. garlic powder
- 1 tbsp. onion powder
- 2 cups beef broth
- 16 oz. elbow macaroni

Ingredients (for sauce)

- 1 cup half and half
- 10 oz. Cheddar cheese (shredded)
- 3 oz. American cheese (cut into strips, from the deli but without cellophane package)
- 2 cups fresh spinach (optional, finely chopped)
- 2 tsps. kosher salt (or to taste)
- ½ tsp. pepper (or to taste)
- Additional shredded cheese (if desired, for garnish)

Instructions

1. Select the "Sauté" function on the display panel.
2. Add the ground beef, garlic powder, and onion powder to the pot and cook. Keep stirring until every pink has disappeared.
3. Stop sautéing by pressing "Cancel" on the pot. Add the elbow macaroni and broth. Firmly secure the lid with the vent valve on closed.
4. Select "Manual or Pressure Cook" on the display panel and program the timer for 4 minutes using the "+/-" keys.
5. When the timer counts down to zero, use the quick release method to allow the pressure to escape.
6. Add half and half and stir well followed by the cheese bit by bit, allowing each bit to melt. Season with pepper and salt to taste.
7. Fold in chopped spinach (if using) just before serving. Add additional cheese (as and if desired) on top for garnish.

Yield: 4 - 6 servings.

Easy Scallops Alfredo

Ingredients

- 1 ¾ cups alfredo sauce (16 oz. jar)
- 2 ½ cups chicken (or vegetable broth)
- ½ tsp. garlic powder
- ½ tsp. dried oregano
- ½ tsp. red pepper flakes
- 12 oz. regular (no-yolk, or gluten-free, dried egg noodles)
- 1 lb. frozen bay scallops

Instructions

1. Pour 1 ½ cups of the alfredo sauce in the Instant Pot. Add the broth, garlic powder, oregano, and red pepper flakes. Stir until smooth. Add the noodles and stir. Add the frozen scallops block right on top. Now tightly lock the lid.
2. If you are using Max Pressure Cooker, "Pressure Cook" with the timer on 3 minutes and the "Keep Warm" setting off.
3. If you are cooking on All Pressure Cooker, use "Meat/Stew" or manual pressure cook on "High Pressure" with the timer on 4 minutes and the "Keep Warm" setting off.
4. Once the timer beeps to indicate the end of cooking time, turn the cooker off and allow the natural pressure release for a minute. Then quickly release the remaining pressure.
5. Open the cooker by unlatching the lid. Add the other ¼ cup of alfredo sauce and put the lid on the pot but without sealing. Leave it for 5 minutes for the noodles to absorb more of the liquid.
6. Then serve hot.

Yield: 4 servings.

Dan Dan Noodles

Ingredients

- 2 tbsps. peanut oil (or vegetable, corn, or canola oil)
- 1 lb. lean pork (ground)
- 2 tbsps. sambal oelek (or hot red pepper sauce, such as Srirachaor less)
- 6 medium scallions (trimmed, thinly sliced)
- 3 medium garlic cloves (peeled, minced, 1 tablespoon)
- 1 tbsp. fresh ginger (peeled, minced)
- 2 tbsps. honey
- 2 tbsps. dry sherry (dry vermouth, or water)
- ¼ cup soy sauce
- ¼ cup tahini
- 3 tbsps. balsamic vinegar
- 1 tbsp. Worcestershire sauce
- 2 cups chicken broth
- 8 oz. dried spaghetti (broken in half)

Instructions

1. With the timer set for 10 minutes, activate the "Sauté" function.
2. Add the oil and heat for about 1 or 2 minutes. Add the ground pork and stir to break up any clumps. Keep stirring for about 4 minutes or until it turns gray (not brown). Stir in the sambal oelek or hot sauce, scallions, garlic, and ginger. Cook for a few seconds. It should bring out some aroma.
3. Add the honey, sherry (or anything else used), soy sauce, tahini, vinegar, and Worcestershire sauce. Stir well so that the tahini will blend well in the mixture. Add the broth and stir well.
4. Cancel "Sauté" function to stop sautéing. Stir in the spaghetti. Let the noodles submerge in the sauce. But they should not touch the bottom of the pot. Tightly lock the lid.
5. If you are cooking on the Max Pressure Cooker, set the timer for 4 minutes while you cook on "Max" pressure. "Keep Warm" setting should be off.
6. If you are cooking on All Pressure Cooker, cook on "Manual" and set the timer for 6 minutes. "Keep Warm" setting should be off.
7. Once the timer has counted down to zero, do a quick pressure release for the pressure to come back to normal. Unlatch the lid to open the lid on the cooker.
8. Stir well and serve.

Yield: 4 servings.

SIDE DISHES RECIPES

Brussels Sprouts With Balsamic Vinegar

Ingredients

- 25 Brussels sprouts (about ¾ pound, halved lengthwise)
- 1 cup of water
- 1 tbsp. extra-virgin olive oil
- 2 garlic cloves (finely chopped)
- 1 tbsp. balsamic vinegar
- 1 tsp. kosher salt
- ½ tsp. black pepper (freshly ground)
- 1 tbsp. sesame seeds (roasted)

Instructions

1. Pour the Brussels sprouts in a steamer basket. Add water into the insert of the Instant Pot and position the trivet inside. Place the steamer basket on the trivet. Then cover the pot and tightly lock the lid. Select "Steam" function and use "+/-" keys to program cooking to 1 minute. Ensure that the steam release valve is set to "Sealing".
2. When the cooking stops, do a quick pressure release. Unlatch to remove the lid. Then transfer the Brussels sprouts to a serving plate, using tongs and discard the water. Dry the inner pot with a clean dishcloth.
3. To make the sauce, select "Sauté" on the pot display panel and add oil to sauté for 1 minute. Add the Brussels sprouts, garlic, pepper, and salt, and sauté.
4. Serve hot, sprinkled with the sesame seeds.

Yield: 4 servings.

Couscous With Figs and Almonds

Ingredients

- 2 cups couscous
- ½ cup almonds (slivered toasted)
- ¼ tsp. dried cinnamon
- ½ cup dried figs (sliced)
- 1 tsp. dried mint
- 2 tbsps. dried onion
- 1 tsp. sea salt
- 4 cups vegetable broth (or water)

Instructions

1. Combine all dry ingredients in a layer in a jar.
2. All ingredients in the jar into an Instant Pot and add 4 cups of broth or water. Stir well to mix.
3. Tightly cover the lid, ensuring that the vent valve "Sealed". Cook on "High Pressure" for 3 minutes. Allow 5 minutes for the natural steam release and do a manual release of any remaining pressure.
4. Serve.

Yield: 4-6 servings.

Vortex Plus - Dehydrated Spiced Cauliflower "Popcorn"

Ingredients

- 1 - 2 lbs. head of cauliflower
- 2 tbsps. hot sauce like buffalo sauce or Frank's
- 1 tbsp. oil
- 1 tbsp. lime juice
- 1 tbsp. smoked paprika
- 1 tsp. cumin
- ½ tsp. nutmeg

Instructions

1. Chop the cauliflower heads into bite-sized florets.
2. Combine cauliflower and the remaining ingredients in a large bowl. Toss to coat evenly.
3. Divide the cauliflower mixture evenly onto cooking trays in a layer.
4. Position the drip pan at the bottom of the cooking chamber. Insert two cooking trays, on in the top-most position, and the other in the bottom-most position.
5. Select "Dehydrate" on the display panel at the temperature adjusted to 130 degrees and the time set to 1 2 hours. Then press "Start."
6. At the end of the "Dehydrate" program, remove the popcorn.
7. Serve immediately.

Yield: 2-4 servings.

Frijoles Borrachos (Drunken Beans)

Ingredients

- 6 slices bacon (cut into 1-inch strips)
- ½ medium yellow onion (finely chopped)
- 3 serrano chili (finely chopped)
- 2 cloves garlic (minced)
- 1 lb. pinto beans (dried)
- 6 - 8 sprigs cilantro
- 12 oz. Mexican beer (1 bottle)
- 1 ½ - 2 tsps. coarse salt

Instructions

1. Start the Instant Pot on "Sauté" mode to be adjusted to "More or High." Add the bacon to the pot and Fry for 4 to 6 minutes for it to cook through.
2. Add onion, chili, and garlic and allow it to continue on the "Sauté" mode for 2 to 3 minutes more, or until the onion becomes translucent.
3. Add the beans, beer, cilantro, and water enough to reach the mark of two-thirds inside the Instant Pot.
4. Tightly close the lid and set the release valve to "Sealed." Then start cooking on "Manual" and use "+/- " keys to program the cooking to 60 minutes on high pressure.
5. At the completion of the cooking, allow the natural pressure release and release any remaining pressure quickly before unlatching to open the cover of the pot.
6. Season the beans with salt and spoon into bowls.
7. Serve in a plate as a side.

Yield: 8-10 servings.

Horta (Greens) and Potatoes

Ingredients

- 2 bunches greens (dandelion, kale, mustard greens, spinach, Swiss chard, to be washed and chopped)
- 5 in potatoes (washed and cut into large pieces)
- 1 cup of water
- 1 cup olive oil extra virgin
- 1+ lemon juice (plus extra slices, for serving)
- 10 cloves garlic (chopped)
- ½ tsp. pepper
- ½ tsp. salt

Instructions

1. Wash well the combination of greens and chop.
2. Wash the potatoes and chop.
3. Peel the garlic and chop.
4. Combine everything in the Instant Pot, stir very well.
5. Tightly lock the lid to cover the Instant Pot well the vent valve set to "Sealing".
6. Select "Manual or Pressure Cook" use "+/- " keys to program the cooking to 15 minutes.
7. Once the beeps to indicate the end of cooking, quick release the pressure.
8. Serve and enjoy!

Yield: 4-8 servings.

Parmesan Puffs 4 Ways

Ingredients (for parmesan puffs 4 ways)

- 2 egg whites
- 4 oz. good quality parmesan (finely grated)
- 1 cup of water

Ingredients (to finish)

- 1 tbsp. everything bagel seasoning (or poppy seed, or sesame seed mix)
- 1 tbsp. bacon (very finely chopped)
- 1 tbsp. paprika
- 1 tbsp. pecans (very finely chopped)
- 1 cup of water

Instructions

1. Combine egg whites and parmesan in a medium bowl thoroughly for it to resemble loose mashed potatoes.
2. Form the mixture into 8 balls and refrigerate to allow it firm; for at least 30 minutes.
3. Roll parmesan balls in each of the 4 toppings, that is, bagel seasoning, bacon, paprika, and pecan.
4. Place the topped parmesan balls in a steamer basket lined with parchment.
5. Pour the water in the Instant Pot. Insert the steam rack and carefully place the steamer basket on to the steam rack.
6. Tightly secure the lid to cover the pot well, ensuring that the vent is closed.
7. Use the display panel to select the "Manual or Pressure Cook". Program the pot for 5 minutes of cooking time.
8. At the end of the cooking time, quick-release the pressure.
9. Serve warm.

Yield: 4 servings.

Vortex Plus - Perfect Kale Chips

Ingredients

- 8 oz. bunch of curly kale (central vein removed, torn into 2-inches pieces)
- 1 tbsp. olive oil
- 2 tsps. everything bagel seasoning (or 1 tsp. kosher salt)

Instructions

1. Rinse and dry thoroughly the kale using a salad spinner. You can also use a clean dish towel.
2. In a large bowl, drizzle olive oil on the kale and sprinkle with everything bagel seasoning or salt.
3. Thoroughly rub the oil into kale, have leaf coated evenly with oil and seasoning.
4. Then divide the kale onto the cooking trays.
5. Position the drip pan in the cooking chamber at the bottom and select "Airfry" on the display panel. Then set the temperature to 340°F and program cooking for 7 minutes and start airfrying the chips.
6. When the message "Add Food" displays on the panel, insert cooking trays; one in the top-most position and one the other in the bottom-most position.
7. When the message "Turn Food" displays on the panel, remove any chips that are about to brown and toss the contents of each tray. Then interchange the positions of the trays.
8. At the end of the "AirFry" program, remove the chips and serve.

Yield: 2 - 4 servings.

CHAPTER 15: BROTHS, STOCKS, AND SAUCES RECIPES

Broths, Stocks, and Sauces have always been a tasty delight even before the advent of various modern cooking technologies including pressure cooking. But for those have had tastes of food cooked in the Instant Pot, broths, stocks, and sauces cooked elsewhere are not as satisfactory. You too would agree with that if you have had an opportunity to compare and contrast. If not, we have 13 of such recipes here for your trial.

Butternut Squash Bisque

Ingredients

- 2 lbs. frozen butternut squash (peeled, seeded ½ -1-inch cubes)
- 2 cups broth (vegetable or chicken)
- ¼ tsp. nutmeg (grated or 1/8 tsp. nutmeg, ground)
- 2 tsps. thyme leaves (freshly stemmed or 1 tsp. dried thyme)
- ½ tsp. table salt
- ½ cup heavy (or light but not fat-free cream)
- 1 cup whole (or low-fat) milk
- 4 tbsps. butter (½ stick)
- 2 tbsps. all-purpose flour

Instructions

1. Add the squash cubes, broth, nutmeg, thyme, and salt together in an Instant Pot and stir to mix. Tightly lock the lid to cover the pot well.
2. If you are cooking on Max Pressure Cooker, set the timer for 4 minutes and the have the "Keep Warm" setting off.
3. If you are cooking on All Pressure Cookers, cook on "Pressure Cook or Manual" and select "High Pressure" with the timer set for 5 minutes and the "Keep Warm" setting off. Make sure that vent valve is closed.
4. At the end of cook time do a quick release of pressure for the pot's pressure to return to normal. Unlatch the lid to open the pot. Stir in the cream and milk.
5. In an immersion blender, puree the soup while still in the pot. (You may pour the soup in a covered blender and puree in 2 or 3 batches. (To avoid a buildup of pressure while pureeing, remove the knob from the lid of your blender and cover the opening with a thick clean towel so that you do not get burned due to the spewing of hot soup.) If you use a covered blender, return the soup to the pot after blending.

6. Start "Sauté" function on "Low," "Less," or "Custom 250°F" with the timer set for 5 minutes.
7. Keep stirring often as you bring the soup to a simmer.
8. In the meantime, melt butter in a microwave-safe bowl or another container on high in the microwave and in 5-second increments. Stirring flour using a fork to form a thin paste.
9. Whisk the butter mixture into the cooker as the soup simmers. Do not stir. Continue to whisk for about 1 minute until the soup becomes slightly thick.
10. Stop the "Sauté" function and leave the soup to cool to warm. Then serve.

Yield: 4 - 6 servings.

Lazy Day Beef Stew (Fresh or Frozen Beef)

Ingredients

- 1 large onion (chopped)
- 3 cloves garlic (minced)
- 2 tbsps. soy sauce
- 1 ½ cup beef (or chicken broth)
- 1 tbsp. brown sugar
- 1 tbsp. vinegar any kind
- ½ tsp. pepper
- 1 tsp. salt
- 1 - 1.5 lbs. stew beef (fresh or frozen)
- 2 to 3 carrots (cut into 1-inch pieces)
- 3 - 4 red-skinned potatoes (cut into 1-inch pieces)
- 1 cup frozen peas
- 2 tbsps. cornstarch
- 3 tbsps. of water
- 2 tbsps. fresh parsley (optional, chopped)

Instructions

1. In an Instant Pot, add the stew beef and toss in all ingredients listed before it. Tightly close the lid and check to be sure the valve vent is on "Sealing." Start the cooker on "Pressure Cook or Manual" and set the timer for 25 minutes using the "+/–" button.

2. Meanwhile, chop the carrots and potatoes into 1-inch pieces (you may or may not remove the skins). Stir the cornstarch into water and stir until it is smooth to make a slurry.

3. Once the pot beeps to indicate the end of cooking time, allow a 10-minute of natural pressure release. Then do a quick release of the remaining pressure by flipping valve to "Venting".

4. Open the pot when the pin drops and toss in the carrots and potatoes and gradually push them into liquid. Return the cover and tightly latch again. Then select "Pressure Cook or Manual" and set the timer for 4 minutes. This time do a quick release after the 4 minutes and open the pot when the drops.

5. Select "Cancel" and start sautéing. Stir well the cornstarch slurry and gradually stir in about a half of it into the boiling stew. Allow it to continue boiling and add more slurry to your desired thickness.

6. Select "Cancel" to stop sautéing. You can now stir in the frozen peas. Cover but don't seal and let the heat of the stew cook them to a normal degree without turning to mush. Add more pepper and salt to taste if needed. Add the optional parsley.

7. Ready to serve.

Yield: 4 servings.

Mini-Meatball Broth

Ingredients (for the meatballs)
- ½ cup plain bread crumbs
- ¼ cup Parmiggiano Reggiano (ground)
- 1 lb. veal (ground)
- 1 egg (beaten)
- Pepper (to taste)
- Salt (to taste)

Ingredients (for the vegetable stock)
- 6 cups of water
- 1 stalk of celery (cut in half)
- 2 medium potatoes whole
- 2 carrots (peeled)
- 1 onion (halved)
- 3 tomatoes (halved)
- 2 tsps. salt
- 2 tbsps. olive oil
- 2 tbsps. balsamic vinegar
- 8 oz. pastina

Instructions
1. Mix the breadcrumbs, cheese, egg, veal, pepper, and salt with water in a large or medium mixing bowl.
2. Use a melon baller to measure out the right amounts of the meat mixture to form little meatballs. (They should be about the half of your desired size because they will be puffed up to almost double when pressure cooked.)
3. To make vegetable stock, add all of the vegetables with water and salt in the pot. Tightly close the lid of the pressure cooker and cook on "High". After about a few minutes when the pot has reached the pressure peak, reduce the heat to the minimum and cook for about 7-10 minutes.
4. Do the quick pressure release when the cooking time is up.
5. Gently take out all the vegetables except tomatoes and place the rest on a serving dish. Remove and discard any likely floating tomato skin.
6. Taste the broth and see if you need to add more pepper and salt according to taste.
7. Add carefully the meatballs into the hot vegetable broth.
8. Latch the lid of the pot and cook on "High Heat." When the cooker reaches pressure, lower the heat to the minimum and cook on low heat for 5-7 minutes under pressure.
9. Do a quick release of pressure when the time is up.
10. Put the pressure cooker off and add the pastina. Cover and boil according to the package instruction but with one minute less because it will continue to cook and soften as you serve the dish.

11. Meanwhile, to make a vinaigrette with the balsamic vinegar and olive oil, put them in a small vase and shake vigorously. Add previously cooked vegetables as a side dish.

12. When the pastina cook time is up, turn the heat off and serve the mini meatball soup.

Yield: 4 - 6 servings.

Hip Bone Broth

Ingredients

- 6 cups of water
- 1 tsp. apple cider vinegar
- 1 yellow onion (peeled and halved)
- 1-inch ginger (sliced into rounds)
- ½ cup of mushrooms (such as any of shiitake, oyster, or porcini, dried)
- 3 - 4 lbs. mixed bones

Instructions

1. Press the "Sauté" button on the pot's display panel. Add the vinegar and water to the Instant Pot.
2. Add bones, ginger, mushrooms, and onions, to the boiling water. Then carefully add bones to avoid splashing yourself with boiling water. You may immerse each bone halfway before dropping it in the water.
3. Close the pressure cooker by latching the lid. Then select "Manual" cook and allow the default "High" pressure and time "30 minutes".
4. When the cooking program ends, allow the natural release of pressure for 20 minutes as the cooker enters "Keep Warm" mode or "L00:20" on the display panel.
5. Repeat the cooking cycle and steps for two more times. This makes a total of cook and cool time of 150 minutes.
6. At the end of third cooking, after the natural pressure release, open the pot, strain the broth and serve or store.

Yield: 4 - 6 servings.

Mushroom Stock

Ingredients

- 1 oz. porcini mushrooms (dried)
- 1 oz. shiitake mushrooms (dried)
- 16 oz. white mushrooms cremini (fresh, or portobello mushrooms, to be diced)
- 1 large onion (to be diced)
- 1 carrot (to be peeled and diced)
- 2 cloves garlic (chopped)
- 1 leek (green part only, to be well rinsed)
- 1 cup red wine
- 2 tbsps. soy sauce
- 1 bay leaf
- 3 sprigs thyme (fresh)
- 2 sprigs parsley (fresh)
- 1 tsp. black peppercorns
- 12 cups of water

Instructions

1. Soak the dried porcini and dried shiitake mushrooms in 4 cups of hot water.
2. Meanwhile, add fresh white mushrooms and onions to the inner pot of the Instant Pot. Sauté the mushrooms and onions to shrink and soften.
3. Then add the carrot, garlic leek, and wine. Stir well for the wine to evaporate and no longer smells as pungent.
4. Add all other ingredients.
5. Press "Cancel" to stop sautéing. Close tightly the lid of the Instant Pot by latching. Select "Manual" and leave it for 30 minutes default pressure cooking time.
6. When the timer counts down to zero, allow the natural pressure release and wait until the pin drops. Then remove the lid, and use the sieve, nut milk bag, or a strainer to strain the stock.
7. Use immediately or refrigerate when cool for 1 week or freeze for 2 months.

Yield: 6 servings.

Yak and Root Vegetable Stew

Ingredients

- 1 tbsp. olive oil
- 1 lb. grass-fed Yak (diced)
- ½ lb. carrots (peeled and chopped)
- ½ lb. parsnips (peeled and chopped)
- 2 onions (chopped)
- 1 medium sweet potato (peeled and chopped)
- 3 cups bone broth
- ¼ cup apple cider vinegar

Instructions

1. Start the Instant Pot on the "Sauté" mode and pour the oil to heat.
2. Add the Yak to the heated oil.
3. Sauté the Yak until it all sides turn golden brown.
4. Add the remaining ingredients and close. Select the "Soup" option on the pot and cook on high pressure for 30 minutes.
5. Allow the steam to release naturally.

Yield: 4 servings.

Vegetable Broth / Sipping Broth

Ingredients

- 1 - 2 tbsps. oil (optional)
- 1 ½- inch piece ginger (crushed)
- 8 - 10 garlic (crushed)
- ½ cup cilantro (tightly packed)
- 10 mint leaves (chopped)
- ½ tsp. soy sauce (or 2 tsps. miso paste)
- Water
- 1 whole lemon (juiced)

Vegetables (or of your choice)

- ½ cabbage (chopped)
- 1 carrot (sliced)
- ¾ cup corn
- 1 bunch green onion (chopped)
- 1 cup winter melon pieces
- 1 sweet onion (chopped)
- 2 serrano pepper
- 1 cup pumpkin pieces
- 2 tomatoes (chopped)

Spices (or any of your choice)

- 1 tsp. black pepper
- 1 tsp. coriander seeds
- 2 tsps. cumin seeds
- Salt to taste

Instructions

1. Start an Instant Pot on the "Sauté" mode.
2. If you want some nice flavor, you may add oil and let heat it.
3. Add garlic and ginger and fry for 2 minutes.
4. Then add all of the vegetables, fry and stir occasionally for 3-5 until they roast.
5. Add cilantro, mint leaves, and spices.
6. Add soy sauce or its substitute. Mix thoroughly.
7. Pour water but should not exceed the marked maximum level on the pot.
8. Add the lemon juice and stir well.
9. Stop sautéing. Seal well and do manual cooking for 25 minutes.
10. After the cooking time ends, do the natural pressure release (it is dangerous to do a quick release here).
11. Use the sieve or something else to strain the broth and store in the fridge for 3 to 4 days. You can also freeze for up to 2-3 months.

Yield: 6 - 8 servings.

Chicken Stock

Ingredients

- 2 ½ lb. chicken carcasses
- 1 tbsp. oil (optional)
- 2 onions (diced, layers also to be kept)
- 2 celery stalks (diced)
- 2 carrots (diced)
- 2 bay leaves
- 4 garlic cloves (crushed)
- 1 tsp. peppercorn (whole)
- 10 cups of water
- Herbs (fresh, of your choice)
- 1 tbsp. apple cider vinegar (optional)

Instructions

1. Start the Instant Pot on the "Sauté" mode and add the tablespoon of oil. When hot, add the chicken carcasses to brown it on all sides. (This is optional but it can slightly increase the flavor of your stock and give it a kind of brown coloration.)
2. Stop sautéing by pressing "Cancel" and 1/3 cup of water to the pot to deglaze it by scrapping the brown bit from the bottom with a wooden spatula. Pour everything in a medium or large bowl and set aside.
3. Then combine all other ingredients in the pot.
4. Latch the lid over the pot with the vent on "Sealing", set to cook on "Manual" with the pressure on "High" for at least 1 hour. When the cooking time is up, allow a natural pressure release.
5. Unlatch and open the lid to strain the stock using a colander and set it aside to cool. Discard the solids.
6. After cooling, refrigerate the stock for at least 2 hours for the fat to gather and form a layer of gel on the top.
7. Skim off the fat and use immediately. You can also store in the fridge for up to 7 days or in the freezer for up to 2 months.

Yield: 4 servings.

Frijoles de la Olla

Ingredients

- 1 tsp. sea salt
- 2 tbsps. dried garlic
- 1/3 cup dried onion
- 2 tsp. Mexican oregano (dried)
- 3 cups pinto beans (dried)
- 6 cups vegetable broth (or water)

Instructions

1. Prepare the ingredients by layering everything in a jar one after the other.
2. Pour all the combined ingredients into an Instant Pot and add the vegetable broth or water.
3. Stir well to mix.
4. Secure the lid with the vent in the "Sealing" position. Set to "Pressure Cook" on high with the timer on 30 minutes.
5. After cooking time, allow the natural steam release for 20 minutes and open the lid.
6. Then serve immediately.

Yield: 6 - 8 servings.

Chicken Bone Broth

Ingredients

- 4 lbs. mixed bones
- 2 tbsps. extra-virgin olive oil (optional)
- 4 carrots halved (crosswise)
- 2 stalks celery (halved, crosswise, with leaves)
- Black pepper (freshly ground, optional)
- Fine sea salt
- 4 cloves garlic (crushed)
- 1 large yellow onion (quartered)
- 1 bunch flat-leaf parsley
- 1 tbsp. apple cider vinegar
- 6 - 8 cups water (filtered)

Instructions

1. If you are using the cooked bones, place them right away in the Instant Pot insert.
2. If you are using raw bones, set them on a baking sheet and drizzle with the oil (if using). Season them with the black pepper and sea salt. Meanwhile, preheat the oven to 400°F and roast the bone for 20 minutes. Then transfer the roasted bones and any yielded juices to the Instant Pot.
3. Add the carrots, celery, garlic, onion, parsley, apple cider vinegar, and filtered water enough to slightly immerse the bones.
4. Tightly secure the lid. Select the "Soup/Stew" option and cook for 80 minutes. After the cooking has stopped, do a natural pressure release for 20 minutes and quick release the remaining pressure.
5. Open the lid and add the broth fat into the pot, sieving it through a fine mesh so that the bone particles and other particles are strained off.
6. Use immediately.
7. If you want to use it in the future, allow the broth to cool down to room temperature. Pour into airtight containers and store in the fridge for up to a week. When you are ready to use, reheat in a saucepan for 15 minutes, over medium-low heat, or until heated through.

Yield: 8 - 10 cups.

Mexican Caldo de Res

Ingredients (for first cooking cycle)

- 1 lb. pound beef stew meat
- ½ cup cilantro (chopped)
- 2 tbsps. garlic (minced)
- 2 tsps. ground cumin
- 1 cup onion (chopped)
- 2 tsps. salt
- 5 cups of water

Ingredients (for second cooking cycle)

- (8 cups, total mixed vegetables)
- ¼ cabbage (cut into wedges)
- 1 carrot (sliced)
- 1 ear corn (cut into 1-2-inch rounds)
- 8 red potatoes (cut in half)
- 1 chayote squash (cut into 2-3-inch pieces. You can use substitutes like zucchini. If using zucchini, do not pressure cook with other vegetables).

Instructions

1. Add all ingredients for the first cooking cycle together in the Instant Pot. Set to cook on "High Pressure" and the timer for 20 minutes. When it beeps after 20 minutes, do a quick pressure release.
2. Add all vegetables for the second cooking cycle to the pot and set to cook at "High Pressure" with the timer on 5 minutes this time. Again, do a quick pressure release when time is up.
3. You can add additional salt or water if needed. If not, serve immediately.

Yield: 8 servings.

Vegetable Stock

Ingredients

- 2 carrots (peeled, chopped)
- 2-3 ribs celery (chopped)
- 1-2 cloves garlic (chopped)
- 1 leek (green part only, well rinsed and chopped)
- 2 bay leaves
- 1-2 onions (chopped)
- 3-4 sprigs parsley
- 1-2 sprigs rosemary
- 1 tsp. black peppercorns
- 1-3 sprigs thyme
- 12 cups of water

Instructions

1. Combine all ingredients in the Instant Pot inner pot and mix well.
2. Tightly secure lid in place with the vent valve on "Sealing." Set it "Manual" cooking for 30 minutes.
3. After the cooking time has elapsed, allow it to do the natural pressure release.
4. Use a sieve or nut milk bag, or a strainer to strain the stock.
5. Ready to use immediately. It can be stored for up to a week in the fridge or 3 months in the freezer.

Yield: 6 servings.

Kimchi Beef Stew (Kimchi Jjigae)

Ingredients

- 1 lb. beef (cut into 2-inch cubes, fatty cut preferably)
- 2 cups prepared kimchi
- 2 cups of water
- 1 cup yellow onions (chopped)
- 1 cup dried shiitake mushrooms (or other dried mushrooms)
- 1 tbsp. garlic (minced)
- 1 tbsp. fresh ginger (minced)
- 1 tbsp. sesame oil (toasted)
- 1 tbsp. dark soy sauce
- 1 tbsp. gochugaru Korean ground red pepper (or ½ tsp. cayenne pepper)
- 1 tbsp. gochujang Korean red chili paste
- ½ tsp. sugar
- Salt (to taste)
- 1/2 cup Sliced scallions for serving
- 1 cup diced firm tofu for serving (optional)

Instructions

1. Combine all other ingredients, apart from the salt, scallions, and tofu in the Instant Pot.
2. Tightly latch the lid on the pot ensuring the pressure release valve is on "Vent". Set at "Manual or Pressure Cook" and cook at "High Pressure" with the timer set 15 minutes.
3. When the timer beeps to show the end of cooking, leave the pot for the natural release of pressure.
4. Add in salt if as needed. If using scallions, serve by stirring them in with the tofu.

Yield: 6 servings.

CHAPTER 16: SOUPS RECIPES

Soups cooked on the Instant Pot usually retain all that has been put together in them. None of the ingredients that make up such soups will be found missing. The contribution of all of them always makes a great soup that can be drunk or used as topping or side for any food. You may get this clearer after going through 13 recipes of such soup listed here.

Tater Tot Soup

Ingredients

- 6 cups broth (chicken or vegetable) 1 ½ quarts
- 2 tbsps. butter
- 2 tsps. dried basil oregano (or thyme)
- 2 tsps. garlic (peeled, minced)
- 1 tsp. onion powder
- ½ tsp. black pepper (ground)
- 1 lb. hash brown cubes (frozen, unseasoned, 3 cups)
- 5 cups frozen Tater Tots (or potato puffs; 1 ¼ lbs.)
- 2 cups cheddar cheese (shredded mild or sharp; 8 oz.)

Instructions

1. Start the "Sauté" function on the Instant Pot and adjust it to "High" or "More" or "Custom 400°F" and the time to 10 minutes.

2. Pour the broth into the pot and add butter, dried herb, garlic, onion powder, and pepper. Stir occasionally as it continues to heat until the steam wisps rise from the liquid. Then add the hash brown cubes and frozen Tater Tots. Tightly secure the lid onto the pot.

3. If you are cooking with Max Pressure Cooker, cook for 3 minutes while the "Keep Warm" setting is adjusted to off.

4. If you are cooking with All Pressure Cooker, select the "Soup/Broil" or "Pressure Cook/Manual" and choose "High Pressure" with the time set to 4 minutes and "Keep Warm" is adjusted to off. Ensure that the vent valve is closed.

5. When the time is up, quickly release the pressure. When the pot's pressure is back to normal, unlatch the lid and open the cooker. Then stir in the cheese and wait for a couple of minutes for it to melt while the lid is askew over the Instant Pot.

6. Stir thereafter and then serve hot.

Yield: 6 - 8 servings.

Tortilla Soup

Ingredients

- 2 ¼ cups red enchilada sauce (19-oz. can)
- 2 cups broth (chicken or vegetable)
- 1 tsp. thyme leaves (stemmed fresh; or ½ tsp. dried thyme)
- ½ tsp. ground cinnamon
- ½ tsp. ground cumin
- 6-8 frozen quesadillas (of any flavor)

Instructions

1. Start the "Sauté" function on the Instant Pot and adjust it to "High" or "More" or "Custom 400°F" and the time to 10 minutes.
2. Combine all ingredients except the quesadillas in an Instant Pot. Stir occasionally as it continues to heat until the steam wisps rise from the sauce. Then add the frozen quesadillas to the pot while they are not to be pushed to the bottom. Also the sauce may not cover the top of some of them. Tightly secure the lid to cover the pot.
3. If you are cooking with Max Pressure Cooker, cook for 5 minutes while the "Keep Warm" setting is adjusted to off.
4. If you are cooking with All Pressure Cooker, select the "Soup/Broil" or "Pressure Cook/Manual" and choose "High Pressure" with the time set to 8 minutes and "Keep Warm" is adjusted to off. Ensure that the vent valve is closed.
5. When the chosen time ends, quickly release the pressure. When the pot's pressure is back to normal, unlatch the lid and open the cooker. Cut up the quesadillas using cleaned kitchen shears or roughly shred them by pulling them with two forks.
6. To serve the soup, scoop up the broth with bits of the tortillas and filling.

Yield: 6 servings.

Beef and Barley Soup

Ingredients

- 4 oz. cremini mushrooms (trimmed and quartered)
- 1 small onion (cut into ¾-inch pieces)
- 1 ½ tbsp. tomato paste
- 1 tbsp. vegetable oil
- 3 garlic cloves (minced)
- 1 tsp. thyme (minced, fresh; or ¼ tsp. dried)
- ¼ tsp. pepper
- 3 cups beef broth
- 1 carrot (peeled and cut into ¾-inch pieces)
- 1 tbsp. soy sauce
- 8 oz. top sirloin steak (trimmed, cut into ¼-inch pieces)
- ¼ cup barley (quick-cooking)
- 2 tbsps. parsley (minced, fresh)

Instructions

1. Combine mushrooms, garlic, oil, onion, pepper, tomato paste, and thyme in microwave-safe bowl and microwave. Stir occasionally, until the vegetables are softened. This takes about 5 minutes. Then pour all into a blender adding broth, carrot, and the soy sauce. Secure the lid and choose "Soup Program 1" to have chunky soups.
2. Press "Pause" to halt the program when preheating ends. The timer will start the 20-minute countdown. At the end of 20 minutes, carefully remove the lid. Stir in the barley and steak.
3. Then return the lid and latch again. Then resume program. At the end of the processing, season with salt and pepper to taste.
4. While serving, sprinkle with parsley.

Yield: 2 - 4 servings.

Super Greens Soup

Ingredients

- 1 small onion (cut into ¾-inch pieces)
- 1/3 cup Arborio rice
- 2 tbsps. extra-virgin olive oil
- 3 garlic cloves (peeled)
- ¾ tsp. table salt (divided)
- ¼ cup yogurt (whole-milk)
- 1 tsp. tarragon (minced, fresh; or parsley)
- ¼ tsp. finely grated lemon zest (plus ½ tsp. juice)
- 6 oz. Swiss chard (stemmed and chopped)
- 4 oz. kale (stemmed and chopped)
- 1 cup baby arugula

Instructions

1. Combine the broth, garlic, oil, onion, rice, and ½ teaspoon salt in a blender. Secure the lid in place. Then select the "Soup program 2" to have creamy soups.
2. In the meantime, combine in a bowl lemon zest and juice, tarragon, yogurt, and remaining ¼ teaspoon salt. Refrigerate all until ready to serve.
3. When it is 12 minutes before the completion of soup 1 program, pause it. Gently remove lid. Stir in the chard and kale until completely submerged. Then return the lid to secure and resume program.
4. Again pause it 1 minute to the end and carefully remove it. Then stir in arugula and return the lid securely. Resume the final lap of the program.
5. At the end of the soup program, adjust its consistency with extra broth according to the desired taste and season with pepper and salt.
6. While serving, drizzle with yogurt sauce.

Yield: 2 - 4 servings.

Minestrone Soup

Ingredients
- 1 cup kidney beans (dried)
- ½ cup navy beans (dried)
- 4 cups of water (divided)
- 1 tbsp. extra-virgin olive oil
- 2 garlic cloves (finely chopped)
- 3 shallots (finely chopped)
- 1 medium carrot (cut into bite-sized pieces)
- 2 celery stalks (cut into bite-sized pieces)
- 5 white mushrooms (quartered)
- 1 zucchini (cut into bite-sized pieces)
- 2 tsps. kosher salt
- 2 tsps. fresh basil (chopped, divided)
- 1 tsp. dried basil
- 1 tsp. dried oregano
- 1 tsp. freshly ground
- Black pepper
- 1 cup broth (vegetable)
- 1 cup shell pasta

Instructions
1. Soak the kidney and navy beans in a large bowl, submerged up to 2 to 3 inches in cold water at room temperature for at least 8 hours, or overnight if possible. Then rinse and drain.
2. Add the soaked and rinsed beans into the Instant Pot with 3 cups of water. Then tightly lock the lid onto the pot ensuring that the steam release knob is moved to "Sealing". Select "Pressure Cook / Manual" on the display panel and set to cook on "High Pressure." Use "+/-" button to set the timer for 8 minutes. At the end of the pressure cooking time, allow the natural release of the pressure for 5 minutes. Then do a quick pressure release. Unlatch the lid to open the cover.
3. Drain the beans but reserve 1 cup of the bean water. Then wipe dry the inset of the Instant Pot with a clean dishcloth.
4. Start the "Sauté" function on the pot's display and heat the oil. Add garlic, shallots, to the hot oil and cook for 2 minutes. Then add the carrot, celery, mushrooms, and zucchini, celery, carrot and continue sautéing for 1 minute.
5. Add the salt, dried basil, 1 teaspoon of fresh basil, oregano, and pepper. Stir well to combine. Add the reserved bean water and the vegetable broth.
6. Tightly secure the lid by latching on the cover ensuring that the steam release knob is on "Sealing". Select "Soup" and cook on "High" pressure. Use "+/-" button to set

the timer for 5 minutes. Allow the natural pressure release at the end of cooking time. Then unlatch to open the cover.

7. Add the remaining 1 cup of water and the pasta into the pot. Tightly secure the lid by latching on the cover ensuring that the steam release knob is on "Sealing". Lock the lid into place. Select "Pressure Cook / Manual" on the display panel and "High" pressure. Use "+/-" button to set the timer for 5 minutes. Quick-release the pressure at the end of the cooking time.

8. Then unlatch the lid to open the pot.

9. While serving hot, stir the in rest of fresh basil.

Yield: 8 servings.

Lemongrass-Ginger Kabocha Squash Soup

Ingredients

- 1 ½ tbsps. grapeseed oil (or other neutral, high-heat cooking oil)
- 1 large yellow onion (diced)
- 2 medium carrots (diced)
- 4 garlic cloves (minced)
- 2- inch piece ginger (fresh, grated or minced)
- 3 Thai green chili peppers (thinly sliced, seeded for milder heat, or omit entirely)
- 4 cups broth (vegetable, low-sodium)
- 2 large Fuji apples (unpeeled, roughly chopped)
- 1 ½ tsps. kosher salt
- 13.5 oz. coconut milk (full fat, 1 can)
- 1 tbsp. tamari or soy sauce (reduced- sodium)
- 2 pieces lemongrass stalks (tough outer layers to be removed, stalks cut into 6-inch, optional but recommended)
- 1 to 2 tsps. fresh lime juice (or to taste)
- Roasted peanuts (optional)
- Sautéed shiitake mushrooms (optional)
- Fresh cilantro chopped (optional)

Instructions

1. Use a large and sharp knife to cut the squash into 2 through the stem and cut off the stem. (If the squash is too tough, you may microwave it for about 3 minutes so that it can be soft and easy to cut.) Using a large spoon, scoop out seeds and gunk and divide each half into 4 or 5 wedges with each wedge laid flat on the side. Cut and peel them off. Then, cut the squash into chunks of about 1 ½ inches to have 5 cups or so of squash.
2. Select the "Sauté" function on the Instant Pot's display panel and add oil to the hot pot after a couple of minutes. Add the carrots and onion to the hot oil and sauté for 5 minutes. Stir occasionally until the onion starts turning brown. Add the garlic and ginger, and if using, chili and cook for 1 more minute, keep stirring frequently.
3. Deglaze the by pouring in the vegetable broth and using a wooden spoon to scrape up browned bits from the bottom of the Instant Pot. Add the kabocha squash, apples, coconut milk, lemongrass, salt, and tamari. Stir well to combine and cancel sautéing.
4. Tightly close the lid with the release valve on "Sealing." Select the "Soup" option and cook at "High Pressure" with the cook time set 12 minutes.

5. Once the timer beeps signaling the end of cooking time, allow a 5-minute of natural pressure release and move the release valve from "Sealing" to "Venting" for a quick release of the remaining steam.

6. Unlatch the lid and open the pot. Discard the lemongrass stalks and puree the soup in an immersion blender for a couple of minutes to form a creamy and thick soup. (You may equally blend the soup in batches, using a high-powered blender. For this option, remove the center cap from the blender lid avoid a buildup of pressure. Instead, cover the hole with a kitchen towel.)

7. Stir in 1 teaspoon of lime juice. Taste, and if needed, add another teaspoon. Also, adjust the seasonings to taste. Then serve the soup in bowls and garnish to taste.

Yield: 4 servings.

Broccoli Cheddar Soup

Ingredients

- 5 cups broth (vegetable or chicken; or water)
- 1 - 2 stalks celery (thinly sliced)
- 1 lb. broccoli (cut in big chunks)
- 2 cloves garlic crushed (optional)
- 1 medium onion (chopped)
- ½ tsp. pepper
- 1 tsp. salt
- 1 tsp. dried basil (or 2 tsps. fresh basil; optional)
- ¼ cup flour
- 2/3 cup of water
- 1 - 2 cup cups cheddar cheese (sharp, grated)
- ½ cup heavy cream (Half & Half or milk)
- 1 tsp. sugar (optional but adds additional flavor)

Instructions

1. Combine the broth or water with 7 ingredients listed after it in the Instant Pot. Tightly latch the lid on the pot, ensuring that the vent valve is set to "Sealing". Press "Pressure Cook / Manual" and set the time to 5 minutes.
2. Meanwhile, combine the flour and water and whisk together until smooth. When the Instant Pot beeps, do a quick pressure release by moving the valve to "Venting". Remove the lid when the pin drops.
3. Select "Sauté" and bring the mixture to boil again, stirring frequently. Whisk for the final time flour and water and pour about half of the slurry of in the soup. Keep stirring until it is boiling and thickens. Add some more slurry for a thicker soup and keep boiling.
4. Puree the soup, using an immersion blender or pour into a food processor and blend safely and then return to the pot.
5. Add the cheese and stir until melted and smooth. Press "Cancel" to turn the pot off. Add the cream (or milk) and sugar. Taste, and if more pepper or salt is needed, add.
6. Serve and a sprinkle with broccoli, cheese, florets or croutons.

Yield: 2 servings.

Vegetable Minestrone With Pasta

Ingredients

- 2 tbsps. extra-virgin olive oil
- 1 medium yellow onion (chopped)
- 4 carrots (peeled and sliced)
- 2 celery stalks (sliced)
- 3 garlic cloves (minced)
- 6 cups vegetable broth (low sodium)
- ½ tsp. black pepper (freshly ground)
- 1 tsp. dried oregano
- ½ tsp. dried thyme
- 1 tsp. fine sea salt
- 2 bay leaves
- 30 oz. red kidney beans (2 cans of 15 oz.; drained, rinsed)
- 30 oz. tomatoes (2 cans of 15 oz.; diced)
- 6 oz. tomato paste (1 can)
- 2 cups dried macaroni pasta (whole-wheat)
- ½ cup parmesan cheese (grated)

Instructions

1. Start the "Sauté" function and add the olive oil to hot the inner pot. Add onion, carrots, celery, and garlic when the oil is hot and let the sautéing continue for 3 minutes for the vegetables begin to soften.
2. Stop sautéing by pressing "Cancel" and add the broth. Using a wooden spoon, deglaze by scraping up any browned bits stuck to the pot's bottom. Add the oregano, bay leaves, pepper, thyme, and salt. Then stir well for all to combine.
3. Add the beans, tomato paste, and diced tomatoes. Don't stir so that tomatoes will not go down and burn.
4. Tightly secure the lid and ensure that the pressure release valve is on "Sealing". Choose "Pressure Cook / Manual" on "High" pressure. Set the timer to 5 minutes. When the pot beeps, allow a natural release of pressure. After 10 minutes, do the quick release of the remaining pressure.

Yield: 6 servings.

Thai Coconut Carrot Soup

Ingredients

- 1 tbsp. coconut oil
- 1 small onion (peeled and diced)
- 1 pound carrots (peeled and diced)
- 1 tbsp. Thai red curry paste
- 2 cloves garlic (minced)
- 4 cups vegetable broth
- 1 cup coconut milk (canned)
- 1 tsp. honey
- 1 tbsp. lime juice
- ¼ tsp. red pepper flakes
- 1 tsp. sea salt
- ½ tsp. black pepper (ground)
- ¼ cup basil (fresh, julienned, plus 3 tbsps. for garnish)

Instructions

1. Start the "Sauté" function and add the coconut oil to hot the inner pot and heat.
2. Add the carrots and onion and continue sautéing for 3-5 minutes more until onions become translucent.
3. Add the curry paste and garlic and continue sautéing for 1 minute.
4. Add the remaining ingredients except for the reserved 3 tablespoons of basil. Lock the lid and tightly close as usual.
5. Select the "Soup" function with the time set to 20 minutes. When timer beeps, allow the pressure to release naturally for 10 minutes. Then quickly release the remaining pressure and let the float valve drop before unlocking the lid.
6. Insert the immersion blender to the Instant Pot and puree the soup. You can also puree in batches using a food processor.
7. Garnish with ½ tablespoon of basil per bowl as you serve.

Yield: 6 servings.

Mushroom Soup

Ingredients

- 1 small onion (diced)
- 8 oz. white button mushrooms (or cremini mushrooms, chopped)
- 8 oz. Portobello mushrooms (about 2 large; with stem and gills removed)
- 2 cloves garlic (minced)
- ¼ cup white wine
- 2 ½ cups mushroom stock
- ¼ tsp. black pepper
- 1 tsp. fresh thyme
- 2 tsp. salt

Ingredients (for cashew cream)

- 1/3 cup raw cashews (soaked if you're not a using high-speed blender)
- ½ cup mushroom stock (or water)

Instructions

1. Combine onion and mushrooms in the inset of the Instant Pot. Start the "Sauté" function to heat all keep stirring every couple of minutes until mushrooms start to shrink and release their liquid, about 10 minutes.
2. Stir in the garlic and sauté 2 more minutes. Then add the wine and continue sautéing until nearly evaporated and reduces the pungency of smell.
3. Add pepper, thyme, salt, and the mushroom stock. Stir well. Cancel sautéing.
4. Tightly close the lid safely as usual. Select "Manual" cook and set the timer for 5 minutes.
5. While cooking is on, add water to the cashew and blend in a high-powered blender until smooth.
6. When the Instant Pot beeps to signal the end of cook time, do the quickly release of the pressure from the Instant Pot. Remove the lid when the pin drops.
7. Carefully pour the soup into the blender with the cashew cream. Blend to desired smoothness and serve.

Yield: 2 - 4 servings.

Thai Red Curry Lentil Soup

Ingredients

- 1 tbsp. coconut oil
- 1 small onion (chopped)
- 2 cloves garlic (chopped)
- 1 tbsp. ginger (grated)
- 1 tbsp. Thai red curry paste (use 2 tbsps. for spicier curry)
- 3 cups broth (chicken or vegetable)
- 13.5 oz. coconut milk (1 can)
- 1 cup red lentils
- ½ head cauliflower (chopped small)
- 2 cups spaghetti squash (cooked)
- 1 tbsp. fish sauce
- Pinch salt
- 1 lime (juiced, plus an additional one to serve)
- Cilantro to serve

Instructions

1. Start the sauté mode to heat the Instant Pot and add the oil when the message "Hot" displays.
2. Add onion to the hot oil and sauté about 3 minutes or until it is translucent.
3. Stir in the garlic and ginger and sauté for 1 additional minute.
4. Stir in the curry paste and sauté for about 30 seconds to 1 minute, maximum to avoid burning it.
5. Pour 1 cup of the broth and stir to mix well with the curry paste and to completely dissolve. Add the rest of the ingredients.
6. Latch the lid firmly with the valve vent on "Sealing" and cook at "High Pressure" with the timer set for 15 minutes. After the end of cook time, wait 10 minutes for the natural pressure release and then do a quick pressure release.
7. Open the pot and use an immersion blender to puree the soup.
8. Serve with a wedge of lime, chopped cilantro. Add fresh chili to have a hot and spicier soup!

Yield: 6 - 8 serving.

Red Pepper Soup with Gouda

Ingredients

- 1.5 lb. red bell peppers (halved; about 4 peppers)
- 1 tbsp. canola oil
- 1 cup onion (diced)
- ½ cup carrot (sliced)
- ½ cup celery (sliced)
- ½ tsp. garlic powder
- 14.5 oz. vegetable broth (1 can)
- 15.5 oz. navy beans (unsalted, rinsed, and drained; (1 can)
- 1 chipotle chili canned (in adobo sauce)
- 1 tsp. adobo sauce
- 1 cup half and half
- 1 ounce Gouda cheese (shredded; about ¼ cup)

Instructions

1. Slice 3 bell pepper halves, and chop 2 halves. Set aside remaining pepper halves and the chopped one.

2. Start "Sauté" function on the Instant Pot left opened. Adjust to "More" mode. When the message "Hot" is displayed on the panel, swirl in the oil. When the oil his thin, add the sliced bell pepper to the cooker and continue sautéing, stirring constantly for 5 minutes or until it turns brown. Press "Cancel" to turn the cooker off.

3. Stir in remaining bell pepper halves, carrot, celery, garlic powder, onion, vegetable broth, chipotle chili, beans, and adobo sauce.

4. Tightly close and latch the pot and ensure that the steam release handle is turned to "Sealing". Select "Manual" "High Pressure," and use the "-/+" button to adjust it to 6 minutes cooking time. When the pot beeps to signify that the time is up, turn the cooker off. Use the natural pressure release method to bring down to pressure before opening the cooker. Take the inner pot out of the cooker and allow it cool for 15 minutes.

5. Meanwhile, pour the half of pepper mixture in a food processor. Remove the lid on top of the blender and replace with a clean kitchen towel so that steam can escape. Blend until smooth and set aside in a large bowl to repeat the process for with the second half.

6. Add the puréed mixture back to the inner pot stir in half-and-half. Start back the "Sauté" function on "More" mode. While the pot is open, sauté for, 3 to 4 minutes or until thoroughly heated.
7. Scoop the soup into bowls and serve with the sprinkle of cheese and bell pepper.

Yield: 6 servings.

Irish Potato Kale Soup

Ingredients

- 2 tbsps. olive oil
- 2 cups leeks (white and light green parts only; thinly sliced; about 1 ½ cm)
- 6 cups vegetable broth (salted)
- 2 lb. potatoes (peeled and diced in ¾-inch cubes)
- 2 cloves garlic (minced)
- 8 oz. kale (with stems and center ribs taken off and leaves chopped)
- ½ tsp. apple cider vinegar
- Black pepper (to taste, freshly ground)
- Green onion (chopped, for garnish)

Instructions

1. Preheat the cooker by pressing "Sauté" and add oil when it gets hot. Add the oil and the leeks to the oil. Sauté for 7-10 minutes for the leeks to soften.
2. Add the vegetable broth, garlic, and potatoes. Tightly lock the lid. Select "Manual" and set the cooking time to 6 minutes.
3. When the pot beeps to signify the end of cooking, do a quick pressure release by setting the steam handle to "Venting" and press "Cancel".
4. Gently mash the potatoes when breaking them as they will be very soft and can fall falling.
5. Stir in the kale and cover back the pot. Select "Manual" and set the timer to 2 minutes.
6. Do a quick pressure release when the pot beeps by moving the steam handle to "Venting". Then select "Cancel" to runt the pot off.
7. Add the apple cider vinegar. Season with salt to taste and grind in black pepper, also to taste.
8. Serve hot, garnishing with the green onion.

Yield: 4 - 6 servings.

CHAPTER 17: PALEO DIET RECIPES

The Paleo diet emphasizes cleanness of recipes and cutting down on oxidation. If you are on the paleo diet or you are cooking it for someone else, you will appreciate keeping your proteins and fats intact and not losing them to cooking. The Instant Pot's power or pressure cooking is made for the instant and intact cooking that help to strictly keep to the paleo diet. This chapter on the Paleo Instant Pot recipes describes flavorful veggies, tender meats, and even wholesome desserts recipes with rich spices, all within minimal cook time.

BBQ Chicken Drumsticks

Ingredients

- 4-10 chicken drumsticks
- ¼ cup sweet paprika
- ¾ cup of water
- 4 ½ tsps. black pepper (freshly ground)
- 1 ½ tsps. celery salt
- 1 ½ tsps. cayenne pepper
- 1 tbsp. salt
- 1 ½ tsps. garlic powder
- 1 ½ tsps. dry mustard
- 1 ½ tsps. cumin (ground)

Instructions

1. Pour ¾ cup of water into the Instant Pot and place the trivet inside.
2. Position the chicken drumsticks carefully on the trivet.
3. Tightly close the lid and shift the vent valve on "Sealing".
4. On the Instant Pot display panel, select "Poultry / Pressure Cook" function and use the "-/+" button to adjust the time to 20 minutes.
5. Meanwhile, preheat the oven to bring to broil.
6. Line a baking sheet with parchment paper.
7. When the timer beeps, allow the pressure to release naturally. Unlatch the lid, open the pot, and transfer the drumsticks to a plate.
8. Coat each drumstick with the BBQ and rub evenly. Then place on the lined cooking sheet.
9. Bring the drumsticks to broil for 2 minutes each side to brown. But it should not be more than that to avoid burning.
10. Serve immediately.

Yield: 4 - 6 servings.

Sriracha Sloppy Joes

Ingredients

- 2 tbsps. neutral vegetable oil (or ghee)
- 1 lb. lean ground beef (preferably 90% lean)
- 1 medium yellow onion (diced)
- 1 large green bell pepper (seeded and diced)
- ¼ cup brown sugar (firmly packed)
- 2 large carrots (diced)
- 2 garlic cloves (chopped)
- 2 tbsps. soy sauce (low-sodium)
- 2 tbsps. sriracha
- 1 cup tomato sauce
- 2 tbsps. rice vinegar
- 4 hamburger buns (split and toasted)
- 1 red onion (thinly sliced; for serving)
- Sandwich pickles (sliced; for serving)

Instructions

1. Start the "Sauté" setting on the Instant Pot and preheat. Add vegetable oil to the pot and add the ground beef to the oil when hot. Continue the "Sauté" function and have the meat cooked through without any traces of pink. That's about 10 minutes. Keep breaking up the meat as it cooks, using a spoon.
2. Add the onion, bell pepper, carrots, and garlic. Then continue sautéing for about 6 minutes more for the vegetable to soften. Stir in the brown sugar, soy sauce, Sriracha, tomato sauce, and vinegar.
3. Tightly secure the lid and shift the pressure release valve to "Sealing". Select "Cancel to program the cooking on "Pressure Cook / Manual" and the time to 20 minutes while the pressure should be high. Then press start. It takes some 10 minutes for pressure to build up.
4. When the timer beeps, you can either do a quick release of pressure by shifting the release valve to "Venting" or leave the pot on "Keep Warm" setting with natural pressure release for up to 10 hours.
5. Stir in the Sloppy Joe mixture. Ladle the mixture onto the hamburger buns. Then top with the red onion and pickles.
6. Serve hot.

Yield: 4 servings.

Coconut Ginger Pork

Ingredients

- 1 tbsp. avocado oil
- 3-4 lb. pork butt/shoulder (roast boneless)
- 1 tsp. ground coriander
- 1 tsp. ground cumin
- 1 tsp. black pepper
- 1 tsp. salt
- 1 onion (peeled and cut into 8 chunks)
- 4 cloves garlic (finely chopped)
- 2- inch piece ginger (peeled and thinly sliced)
- ½ can coconut milk
- Lime wedges (for garnish)

Instructions

1. Start the "Sauté" function on the Instant Pot.
2. Combine the coriander, cumin, pepper, and salt in a container.
3. Using your fingers, rub the mixture over the roast.
4. Add avocado oil to the Instant Pot to coat its bottom and allow it to heat.
5. Place the meat into the oil and add the onion, garlic, ginger, and half can of coconut milk.
6. Program to cook on "High Pressure" with the time set for 45 minutes. (Take note that the amount of broth will be double or triple because the roast will yield its moisture and fat while cooking.)
7. When the cooking ends, do a quick pressure release and unlatch the lid when all the pressure is gone and open the pot.
8. Serve and garnish with lime.

Yield: 3 - 4 servings.

Filipino Chicken Adobo

Ingredients

- 6 chicken drumsticks (or two lbs. of chicken)
- 1 tbsp. oil
- 1 red chili (dried)
- Green onions (chopped; for garnish)
- 10 cloves garlic (crushed)
- 1 tbsp. fish sauce
- ½ cup light soy sauce
- ¼ cup Filipino soy sauce
- 1 tbsp. sugar
- ¼ cup Filipino vinegar
- 1 small onion (minced)
- 1 tsp. black peppercorn (ground)
- 4 bay leaves (dried)
- 1 tsp. cornstarch (mixed with 1 tbsp. water; optional)

Instructions

1. Combine fish sauce Filipino soy sauce, light soy sauce, sugar, and Filipino vinegar in a medium mixing bowl and mix well.
2. Start the Instant Pot on "Sauté" and add oil to the pot when warm. Add the chicken to brown for 1- 2 minutes per side. Remove from the pot and set aside.
3. Add the garlic and onion to the pot and sauté until fragrant and golden. Then, add black peppercorn, chili, and bay leaves to the pot. Allow it sauté for no more than 30 seconds.
4. Add the sauce mixture and deglaze the pot by scraping the brown bit from the bottom.
5. Cook for 9 minutes at "High Pressure".
6. At the end of cook time, do the natural pressure release.
7. You may take the chicken out of the pot and simmer the sauce on "Sauté" mode, adding the cornstarch mixture and sauté until the sauce is reduced.
8. You may also brown the chicken in a broiler for 5 minutes, placing the skin side up.
9. Then place the chicken on a plate and spoon the sauce mixture.
10. Garnish with the chopped green onions and serve.

Yield: 2 - 4 servings.

Kalua Pork

Ingredients

- 2 lbs. pork butt (bone to be removed; cut into large chunks)
- 1 tbsp. smoked sea salt
- 1 tsp. garlic powder
- 1 cup of water
- 1 small cabbage (sliced)

Instructions

1. Sprinkle the pork with sea salt and garlic powder. Rub in thoroughly with hand to coat.
2. Put the pork in the insert of the Instant Pot and add water.
3. Tightly secure the lid, latch the pot, and program to cook on "Manual" with the time adjusted to 90 minutes.
4. When the pot beeps signaling the end of cook time, press "Cancel" to stop cooking and allow the natural pressure release.
5. When all the pressure is released, transfer the pork into a bowl and cover to keep it warm.
6. Add the cabbage to the juices in the pot and stir to coat.
7. Cook on "Manual" with the time adjusted to 3 minutes.
8. When the pot beeps at the end of cook time, allow the natural pressure release.
9. When the pork is somewhat cool, take out the pieces of fat and leave only the meat.
10. Shred the meat and add the cabbage to the meat.
11. Stir to combine.
12. Serve with cauliflower rice and enjoy.

Yield: 4 servings.

Plant-Based Butternut Ginger Bisque

Ingredients

- 1 cup yellow onion (diced)
- 1 green apple (chopped; discard the core and seeds)
- 1 cup carrot (chopped)
- 4 cloves garlic (minced)
- 2 tsps. ginger (peeled and chopped)
- 1 butternut squash (peeled and chopped; about 4 cups)
- 1 tsp. salt
- 2 cups of water
- ¼ cup parsley (finely chopped)
- Black pepper (to taste)

Instructions

1. Start the Instant Pot by pressing the "Sauté" button and bring to hot for 2 minutes. Add the onions to the hot pot and cook for 5 minutes. Add a splash of water as onions start drying up and sticking.
2. Add the next 6 ingredients including and up to the salt; one after the other, stirring as you do.
3. Turn off the Instant Pot by pressing "Cancel". Add water into everything; secure the lid into place ensuring that the nozzle is on "Sealing" position.
4. Set it to cook on "Manual" for 5 minutes.
5. When the timer beeps, do a natural pressure release and allow all pressure to go before unlatching to open the pot. Allow to cool for 10-15 minutes.
6. Pour the soup into the blender in batches and blend until all of the soup is puréed, feeling creamy and smooth.
7. Add the black pepper and parsley and stir well.
8. Serve and enjoy!

Yield: 4 - 6 servings.

CHAPTER 18: VEGAN / VEGETARIAN DIET RECIPES

If beef, chicken, lamb, pork, turkey, seafood, and wild-caught and such things are excluded from your meal, would you still need the Instant Pot? The answer is YES in the affirmative. Note that carefully selected vegan meals can be richly satisfying. Grains and vegetables can be very rewarding. You will how true that is in the following sample of recipes for the vegetarian diet that you will enjoy.

Vegetable Quinoa Tabbouleh

Ingredients

- 2 cups quinoa (rinsed)
- 1 lemon (juiced)
- 1 tbsp. extra-virgin olive oil
- 3 ½ cups of water
- 1 English cucumber (peeled and diced)
- 2 tbsps. fresh mint (chopped)
- ¼ cup (chopped; fresh flat-leaf) parsley
- 1/3 cup pine nuts (toasted)
- 4 scallions (white and light green parts only; chopped)
- 2 medium tomatoes (diced)

Instructions

1. In the inner of the Instant Pot, combine the quinoa, lemon juice, olive oil, and water.
2. Tightly lock the lid and select "Pressure Cook or Manual". Cook on "High Pressure" with the timer set for 20 minutes. Check to see the steam release valve is on "Sealing".
3. When the pot beeps after the cooking, do a quick release the pressure by moving the release valve to "Venting".
4. Unlatch the lid and open the pot. Use a fork to fluff the quinoa, and then stir in the cucumber, mint, parsley, pine nuts, scallions, and tomatoes.
5. Serve immediately. You can also store the tabbouleh using an airtight container in the fridge for up to 4 days.

Yield: 6 servings.

Coconut-Blueberry Chia Pudding

Ingredients

- 14 oz. coconut milk (full fat; 1 can)
- 1 cup of water
- 12 oz. blueberries (frozen; 1 bag)
- 1 cup chia seeds
- 1 cup oats (rolled)
- ½ cup pure maple syrup
- ½ tsp. pure vanilla extract
- Fresh berries for (garnish; optional)

Instructions

1. Combine all ingredients in the inner pot.
2. Tightly lock the lid in place and ensure that the steam release knob on "Sealing". Cook on "Pressure Cook/Manual" and set the time to 3 minutes. Once the pot beeps at the end of the cook time, do the natural release of pressure for 5 minutes. Thereafter, do a quick release of the remaining pressure.
3. Unlatch the lid seal to remove the lid. Share the pudding into different serving cups and keep in the fridge for about 1 hour for it to set. Serve cold, garnishing it with berries. You may also store in an airtight container and keep in the refrigerator for up to 4 days.

Yield: 8 servings.

Israeli Couscous and Lentils

Ingredients (for couscous and lentils)

- 1 cup French green lentils
- 1 medium yellow onion (diced)
- 2 red yellow (or orange bell peppers; diced)
- 2 carrots (diced)
- 6 garlic cloves (minced)
- 1 cup Israeli (or pearl couscous)
- 3 ½ cups vegetable broth (low sodium)
- 2 tsps. kosher salt
- Black pepper (freshly cracked)
- 2 bay leaves
- Handful of fresh thyme sprigs

Ingredients (for finishing)

- 2 ½ tbsps. extra-virgin olive oil
- 1 ½ tbsps. red wine vinegar
- 1 cup fresh dill (finely chopped)
- 1 cup fresh Italian parsley (flat-leaf; finely chopped)
- 15 pitted green olives (sliced)
- 1 pint cherry tomatoes (halved or quartered)
- Kosher salt
- Black pepper (Freshly cracked)

Instructions

1. Soak the lentils for 8 hours or overnight in water. Then drain the lentils.
2. Add the to the Instant Pot the soaked and drained lentils, vegetable broth, bay leaves, onion, bell peppers, carrots, couscous, garlic, pepper, salt, and thyme sprigs. Stir well to combine.
3. Tightly secure the lid and ensure that the steam release valve is set on "Sealing". Set to cook on "High Pressure" for 3 minutes, selecting the "Pressure Cook" setting.
4. Once the timer beeps to show that the cooking is complete, leave for 10 minutes for the natural pressure release. Then switch the release valve to "Venting" for the quick release of the remaining pressure.
5. Open and take the thyme sprigs and bay leaves out from the pot.
6. Add the mixture of couscous and lentil to a large bowl. Allow to cool to the room temperature.

7. Then add the olive oil, dill, parsley, pepper to taste, vinegar, olives, tomatoes, and salt to the lentil and couscous mixture and a splash of vinegar to ensure acidity.

Yield: 4 servings.

Strawberry-Rhubarb Compote

Ingredients

- 1 lb. rhubarb (about 4 large stalks; trimmed and cut into 1-inch pieces)
- 1 lb. strawberries (hulled and quartered lengthwise)
- ½ tsp. ground cardamom
- ½ cup turbinado (or organic cane sugar)

Instructions

1. Combine the rhubarb, with cardamom, sugar, and strawberries in the Instant Pot. Stir well to allow the sugar to evenly coat the rhubarb and strawberries. Set aside for 15 minutes for the fruit releases its moisture. Stir the mixture well so that it can produce more liquid that will be sufficient for the recipe.
2. Tightly secure the lid with the pressure release knob set on "Sealing". Then select the "Manual or Pressure Release" and adjust the cook time to 5 minutes at "Low Pressure." You will wait about 10 minutes before the pot comes to the pressure.
3. Allow about 15 for the natural release of pressure after cooking. Then unlatch and open the pot when the pressure is fully released. Stir your compote for the rhubarb to breakdown completely.
4. Pour the compote into a heatproof container so that it can to thicken as it cools.
5. You can serve warm or chill the compote in the refrigerator. It can stay up to 1 week refrigerated.

Yield: 4 cups.

Vortex Plus Skinny Fries

Ingredients

- 1 lb. russet potatoes (peeled or peeled)
- 2 tsps. olive oil
- Salt to taste

Instructions

1. Using a mandolin slicer, cut the potatoes into ¼-inch sticks and rinse them thoroughly. Then soak the cut potatoes in cold water for 10 minutes or more.
2. Drain the potatoes and pat dry well using a kitchen towel.
3. Toss the potatoes with oil in a large bowl and pour into the rotisserie basket and firmly lock the lid.
4. Position the drip pan at the cooking chamber bottom. Then select the "Airfry" function and adjust the temperature to 380 degrees. Set the time to 20 minutes and then press "Start."
5. When the message "Add Food" is displayed, lift the rotisserie basket into the cooking chamber using the rotisserie fetch tool. Also, using the red rotisserie release lever, secure the basket firmly and close the door. Then select "Rotate."
6. After 17 minutes, check the fries. Remove them when they are golden.
7. Add salt as desired and serve hot.

Yield: 2 - 4 servings.

Massaman Curry With Tofu and Kabocha Squash

Ingredients

- 14 oz. tofu (1 block firm; drained)
- 1 tbsp. coconut oil
- 1 large yellow onion (cut into 1-inch pieces)
- ¼ cup massaman curry paste
- ½ cup coconut cream
- 1 cup vegetable broth (low sodium)
- 1 Kabocha squash (seeded and cut into 1-inch cubes, 1 ½ -pound)
- 1 cup coconut milk
- 1 cup fresh Thai basil leaves (loosely packed)
- Hot steamed rice (for serving)

Instructions

1. Slice the tofu into ½-inch pieces.
2. Sandwich each slice in a single layer to be arranged between double layers of paper towels (you can also use clean sterile folded kitchen towel). Press the tofu firmly to release as much moisture as possible. Then cut the slices into ½-inch cubes and set aside.
3. Set your Instant Pot to "High Sauté". Add the coconut oil to melt. Add the yellow onion and sauté until it starts to brown, about 4 minutes. Add the curry paste and coconut cream and sauté until bubbling and fragrant, that is another 2 minutes.
4. Add the broth and deglaze the pot using a wooden spoon to nudge any browned bits from the bottom. Then add the squash in a single layer.
5. Firmly latch the lid and with the pressure release knob on "Sealing". Select "Cancel" to reset the program. Set to "Manual or Pressure Cook" and adjust the cooking time to 1 minute. Set to cook on "Low Pressure." It will wait for about 10 minutes before coming up to pressure and start the cooking program.
6. At the end of the cooking program, quick-release the pressure by shifting the pressure release valve to "Venting."
7. Then open the pot and add the coconut milk. Stir well and add the tofu. Reset the cooking program by pressing the "Cancel" button. Start the Instant Pot again by choosing "Sauté" program. Allow the curry to simmer, and then cook 2 minutes. Stir gently occasionally to avoid breaking the tofu. End the cooking by pressing the "Cancel" button.
8. Ladle the curry tofu into bowls and serve very hot with the rice.

Yield: 4 servings.

Three-Bean Vegan Chili

Ingredients

- 2 tbsps. chili powder
- 1 tbsp. smoked paprika
- ½ tbsp. ground cumin
- 1 tsp. dried garlic
- ½ tsp. sea salt
- 1/3 cup onion (dried)
- 2 tbsps. celery (dried)
- 2 tbsps. carrots (dried)
- 2 tbsps. mushrooms (such as porcini or shiitake; diced dried)
- 2 tbsps. tomatoes (sundried)
- ½ cup black beans (dried)
- ½ cup pinto beans
- ½ cup great northern (or cannellini beans)
- 6 cups vegetable broth (or water)

Instructions

1. In preparation for cooking, layer the dry ingredients according to the order listed in a jar.
2. Pour all of the ingredients from the jar into the Instant Pot.
3. Add vegetable broth or water.
4. Stir to mix and cover with the lid. Check to be sure that the vent release valve is on "Sealed". Select the "Pressure Cook or Manual" setting and cook on "High Pressure" for 40 minutes.
5. Once the timer beeps to indicate the end of cook time, allow 20 minutes of natural pressure release and do the quick release of the remaining pressure manually.
6. Then serve immediately.

Yield: 6 servings.

Smoky Chipotle Quinoa, Black Beans, and Corn

Ingredients (for dry ingredients)

- 1 tbsp. chipotle powder (ground)
- 2 tsp. cumin (ground)
- 2 tbsps. onion (dried)
- 1 tsp. garlic (dried)
- 1 tsp. Mexican oregano
- ¼ tsp. sea salt
- 2 cups quick-cooking quinoa
- 1 cup black beans (dehydrated)
- ½ cup corn (dried)

Ingredients (for cooking and serving)

- 4 cups vegetable broth (or water)
- Cilantro (roughly chopped, fresh; to serve)
- Lime juice (to serve)

Instructions

1. In preparation, layer all the dry ingredients according to the listed order in a jar.
2. Then pour the ingredient from the jar into the Instant Pot.
3. Add broth or water and stir well to mix.
4. Latch the lid. Check to be sure that the vent release valve is on "Sealed". Select the "Pressure Cook or Manual" setting and cook on "High Pressure" for 5 minutes.
5. Once the timer beeps to indicate the end of cook time, allow another 5 minutes of natural pressure release and do the quick release of the remaining pressure manually.
6. To serve, garnish with cilantro and lime juice.

Yield: 6 servings.

Fruity Quinoa and Granola Bowls

Ingredients

- 1 cup quinoa (rinsed)
- 1 ½ cups of water
- ½ tsp. cinnamon (ground)
- 2 tbsps. maple syrup (plus more for topping; optional)
- 1 tsp. vanilla extract
- Pinch salt
- ½ - 1 cup nondairy milk
- 2 cups granola (any variety)
- 2 cups compote (fresh fruit)
- Bananas (Sliced; for topping; optional)
- Toasted walnuts (for topping; optional)

Instructions

1. Combine the quinoa, water, cinnamon, maple syrup, vanilla, and salt In an Instant Pot.
2. Tightly secure the lid, ensuring that the steam release handle is switched "Sealing." Using the "Manual or Pressure Cook" function, cook on "High Pressure" with the timer set for 8 minutes.
3. Once the timer beeps to indicate the end of cook time, wait 10 minutes for the natural pressure release and do the quick release of the remaining pressure.
4. Remove the lid carefully. Stir the quinoa and enough milk to the desired consistency.
5. Serve the quinoa mix in bowls and top with compote, granola, or/and any other toppings, of your choice.

Yield: 4 servings.

Creamy Veggie Risotto

Ingredients

- 2 tbsps. olive oil
- ½ sweet onion (diced)
- 1 garlic clove (minced)
- 1 bunch asparagus (with tips cut into 1-inch pieces)
- 2 ¾ cups vegetable stock (DIY or store-bought stock)
- 1 cup Arborio rice (rinsed and drained)
- 1 cup sugar snap peas (rinsed, tough ends removed)
- 1 tsp. thyme (dried)
- ½ tsp. salt (plus more as needed)
- ¼ tsp. black pepper (freshly ground)
- Pinch red pepper flakes
- 2 tbsps. vegan butter
- ½ lemon (juiced)
- 1 ½ - 2 cups fresh baby spinach torn

Instructions

1. Start your Instant Pot on "Sauté Low" mode. When the message "Hot" displays, add the oil. Heat until it shimmers and the onion. Sauté for 2 or 3 minutes, stirring frequently. Cancel sautéing by turning off the Instant Pot.
2. Add garlic and asparagus, stir well. Cook again for about 30 seconds.
3. Add the stock, black pepper, and red pepper, peas, rice, thyme, and salt, stirring well with each addition.
4. Tightly secure the lid and turn the steam release handle to "Sealing." Set the pot to the "Manual or Pressure Cook" function and set to cook on "High Pressure" with the timer on 8 minutes.
5. Once the cook time has elapsed, do the quick release of the pressure.
6. Unlatch lid and carefully remove. Stir in the butter, juice, and spinach. Do it carefully to avoid tearing the snap peas.
7. Taste, and if needed, season with more salt or pepper.
8. Serve immediately.

Yield: 4 - 6 servings.

CHAPTER 19: GLUTEN-FREE RECIPES

The Instant Pot is for everybody, including those on dietary restriction. A gluten-free diet is understood to exclude the protein gluten found in such foods as barley, rye, wheat, and so on. It may seem daunting to cut out gluten from your diet. But many healthy, nutritious, and satisfying foods are gluten-free. The following are a few of such foods that can be delicious if you cook them in your Instant Pot.

Spanish Rice With Chorizo

Ingredients
- 2 cups rice (long-grain, like Basmati; to be well rinsed 4 or 5 times)
- 2 - 2 ½ tbsps. olive oil
- 1 large onion (finely diced)
- 3 - 4 oz. chorizo diced (raw or cured)
- 1 tsp. cumin powder
- 2 large cloves garlic (finely diced)
- ½ red bell pepper (diced into small cubes)
- 1 large tomato (diced finely)
- ¼ tsp. salt
- 1 tsp. paprika powder (sweet or regular)
- 1 tsp. vegetable stock (powder or 1 cube)
- 2 - 2 ¼ cups of water

Ingredients (for serving)
- 1 tbsp. olive oil
- ½ red bell pepper (sliced into strips)
- Pinch of salt
- 3 oz. chorizo (sliced)
- 10 - 12 green pitted olives (sliced)

Instructions
1. To reduce the starch contents of the rice, rinse under cold water 4 - 5 times. Set aside.
2. Start the Instant Pot on the "Sauté" function. Add the olive oil to melt. Then add onions, chorizo, and pepper and stir well. Cook for about 5 minutes and stir well once or twice. Then, add garlic and tomatoes and cook for 3 minutes. Add the vegetable stock and the spices. Stir thoroughly to mix well. Then add water and stir in the well-rinsed rice.

3. Stop sautéing by pressing "Cancel". Latch the lid and check to be sure that the pressure release valve is on "Sealing." Select "Manual / High" set the timer for 4 minutes.

4. At the end of the cooking time, wait for 5 minutes for the natural pressure release. Then turn the release valve to "Venting" for the quick release of any remaining pressure.

5. Meanwhile, prepare the ingredients for finishing by heating the oil in a non-stick skillet over medium-high heat. Add the red bell pepper slices and cook for 4 - 5 minutes or until golden brown. Add salt to taste and pour into a bowl.

6. Add the sliced chorizo and cook each side for 2-3 minutes or until it turns brown and crispy.

7. Transfer the rice to a platter and serve with peppers, chorizo, and olive as toppings. A wedge of lemon can also be on the side.

Yield: 4 servings.

Garlic Smashed Potatoes

Ingredients

- 6-8 russet potatoes
- 1 cup of water
- 1 cup whole or raw milk (standard)
- ¼ cup of butter
- 2 garlic cloves (minced)
- 1 ½ tbsps. garlic powder
- 2 tbsps. parsley
- Himalayan salt (to taste)
- Pepper (to taste)

Instructions

1. Place the scrubbed potatoes on the trivet inside the liner of the Instant Pot. Add in the water.
2. Tightly secure the lid by latching it and ensuring that the vent valve is on "Sealing". Select "Manual" cook and adjust the timer to minutes 20 high pressure.
3. When the Instant Pot beeps to show the end of cook time, do the quick pressure release.
4. Use a slotted spoon to transfer the potatoes to a medium mixer bowl and beat for a few minutes to be roughly mixed. (You may use a stand mixer; if you don't have you can use a potato masher or wooden mixing spoon.)
5. Add the remaining ingredients and mix thoroughly.
6. Serve immediately and preserve any leftover for reheating. To reheat, simply spoon a little more milk into the pot and drop the mashed potato. Mix thoroughly while heating until it heats through and mixes well.

Yield: 8 servings.

Refried Beans

Ingredients

- 2 lb. pinto beans (dried, sorted; about 4 - 5 cups)
- 1 ½ cups onion (chopped)
- 4 - 5 garlic cloves (roughly chopped)
- 1 jalapeno (seeded and chopped)
- 2 tsps. dried oregano
- 1 ½ tsps. ground cumin
- ½ tsp. black pepper (ground)
- 3 tbsps. vegetable shortening (or bacon grease/lard for non-vegan)
- 4 cups broth (vegetable; or chicken for non-vegan)
- 4 cups of water
- 1 - 2 tsps. sea salt

Instructions

1. Soak the pinto beans for 15 -20 minutes in a large mixing bowl filled with enough water to submerge the beans by a few inches. Meanwhile, prepare the remaining ingredients.
2. Add the onion, black pepper, cumin, garlic cloves, jalapeno, oregano, vegetable shortening, broth, and water in the Instant Pot bowl and sauté for 3 minutes.
3. Using a colander, strain the beans and throw away the soaking liquid. Again, rinse with water.
4. Cancel sautéing and add the beans to the mixture inside the Instant Pot. Stir everything together and do worry if the vegetable shortening is in a lump, the pressure will melt the fat and it will mix with the liquid.
5. Tightly latch the lid on the Instant Pot, ensuring that the steam release valve on "Sealing". Select "high pressure" and set to cook for 45 minutes.
6. After the cook time, the Instant Pot will do the natural pressure release for 40 minutes if you leave it alone.
7. Then unlatch and open the lid of the Instant Pot and add salt to taste.
8. Using an immersion blender, blend the beans to your desired consistency.
9. They will appear soupy, so wait a few minutes to cool and thicken up.
10. Then serve warm.

Yield: 6 servings.

Chi-Town Italian Beef and Peppers

Ingredients

- ¼ cup olive oil
- 1 tbsp. Italian seasoning
- 1 tsp. garlic powder
- 1 tsp. smoked paprika
- ½ tsp. red pepper flakes
- 1 tsp. salt
- ½ tsp. black pepper (ground)
- 1 green bell pepper (seeded and sliced)
- 1 red bell pepper (seeded and sliced)
- 1 yellow bell pepper (seeded and sliced)
- 1 large yellow onion (peeled and sliced)
- 3 lbs. boneless chuck roasted (quartered)
- 4 cups beef broth
- 1 cup chopped jarred giardiniera (drained)

Instructions

1. Combine oil, garlic powder, smoked paprika, black pepper, red pepper, Italian seasoning, and salt in the Instant Pot. Add green bell peppers and onion to the roast and toss. Put the toast in an airtight container and refrigerate for at least 30 minutes up to overnight.
2. Start the Instant Pot on the "Sauté" function and add meat, vegetables, and marinade. Brown each side of the meat for 5 minutes per side or a little more. Add the broth.
3. Lock lid tightly with the vent released valve closed. Select "Manual/ Pressure Cook" and set the time to 60 minutes on high pressure.
4. When the pot beeps signaling the end of cook time, allow the natural pressure release for 5 minutes. Then turn the vent release valve to the "Venting" for the quick release of the remaining pressure. Wait until the float valve drops and unlock the lid.
5. Use a colander to strain the liquid from the pot while saving ¼ cup and set aside for later use.
6. Set the meat on a cutting board and wait for about 5 minutes. Slice thin the meat and add the vegetables back to the Instant Pot. Also, add the liquid for moistening.
7. Then use a slotted spoon to transfer the meat with veggies into eight bowls and serve with gluten-free buns or/and lettuce wraps while garnishing them with giardiniera.

Yield: 8 servings.

Brussels Sprouts Hash

Ingredients

- 4 slices bacon (quartered)
- 1 medium red (onion peeled and sliced)
- 1 medium sweet potato (peeled and small-diced)
- 1 lb. Brussels sprouts (trimmed and halved)
- 1 cup of water
- 2 tbsps. maple syrup
- 2 tbsps. fresh orange juice
- 1/8 tsp. hot sauce
- 1 tbsp. chives (fresh chopped)

Instructions

1. Start the Instant Pot by pressing the "Sauté" button. Stir-fry the bacon for 5 - 7 minutes or until it turns crisp and fat is rendered. Then transfer the fried bacon to a plate lined with a paper towel. Crumble when cool.
2. Combine the onion, diced potato, and Brussels sprouts in the Instant Pot. Stir-fry for 3 minutes or more in bacon drippings.
3. Add water to Instant Pot, insert the steamer basket, and add vegetables to the pot.
4. Lock the lid tightly and ensure that the pressure release knob is on sealing position.
5. Select "Manual or Pressure Cook" option and use the "+/-" button to set the cook time to 3 minutes.
6. When the timer beeps at the end of 3 minutes, quickly release the pressure and wait for the pin to drop. Then unlock the lid.
7. Pour the veggies into a serving dish and toss with orange juice, maple syrup, and hot sauce. Garnish with crumbled bacon and chopped chives and serve warm.

Yield: 4 servings.

Porcupine Meatballs In Tomato Sauce

Ingredients (for the meatballs)

- 1 lb. ground beef
- 1 large egg (slightly beaten)
- ½ cup yellow onion (finely chopped)
- 1/3 cup Arborio rice
- ¼ cup parsley (chopped fresh)
- Salt (to taste)
- Black pepper (to taste)

Ingredients (for the sauce)

- 14.5 oz. diced tomatoes (1 can undrained)
- 1 cup of water
- 1 tsp. dried oregano
- ½ tsp. cinnamon (ground)
- ½ tsp. paprika (smoked)
- ¼ tsp. cloves (ground)
- Salt (to taste)
- Black pepper (to taste)
- Fresh parsley (chopped; for garnish; optional)

Instructions

1. To prepare the meatballs, combine all meatball ingredients in a large bowl, season with salt and pepper to taste. Mix thoroughly until well combined. Form 8 - 10 meatballs with the mixture and arrange the balls into the Instant Pot in a single layer.
2. To prepare the sauce, combine all the ingredients for the sauce including juices from the tomatoes in a medium bowl and season with pepper and salt. Stir to mix well and pour into the meatballs.
3. Secure the lid tightly on the pot, making sure that the pressure release valve is on "Sealing". Select "Manual / Pressure Cook" and set the Instant Pot to cook at "High Pressure" for 15 minutes.
4. When the machine beeps the end of cook time, leave the pot for another 15 minutes for the natural release of all pressure.
5. Transfer the meatballs gently to a bow.
6. Carefully insert an immersion blender and puree the sauce right inside the pot until the desired smoothness.
7. Then pour the puree over the meatballs.
8. Garnish with parsley, if using, and serve immediately.

Yield: 6 servings.

Curried Chickpeas With Spinach

Ingredients

- 1 cup dried chickpeas (or garbanzo beans; to be rinsed)
- 4 cups of water
- 20 oz. tomato sauce (1 can)
- 1 tsp. garlic powder
- ¼ tsp. ground ginger
- 1 tbsp. curry powder
- 1/8 tsp. ground nutmeg
- ½ tsp. salt
- ¼ tsp. black pepper (ground)
- 2 cups baby spinach (fresh)

Instructions

1. Combine the rinse chickpeas and water in the Instant Pot.
2. Latch the lid and have the release knob point to "Sealing".
3. Press the "Beans" button on the pot and cook for the default 30 minutes.
4. When timer beeps after the 30 minutes, allow the pot to naturally release the pressure for 20 minutes. Then do the quick release of any additional pressure until the float valve drops. Then unlatch and open the lid. If there is any extra liquid, drain it.
5. Add the remaining ingredients and stir well. Adjust the pressure to "Low" and simmer 5 minutes. When it has heated through and spinach has wilted, transfer to a bowl.
6. Serve warm.

Yield: 6 servings.

CHAPTER 20: KETOGENIC DIET RECIPES

The Instant Pot can be a good way for those on special diets like the keto. Apart from helping to retain the original components of the recipes, it improves the tastiness of the final products. For instance, the experience has shown that many of the disadvantages attributed to the ketogenic diet are due to poor processing of foods. If you try the recipes in this chapter in your Instant Pot, you will want to be or remain a ketoer.

Please note that because you must keep the track of your macronutrients when you are on the keto diet, each of the recipes includes the nutritional contents of the meal so that you can evaluate what you are actually cooking.

Steamed Artichoke

Ingredients

- 1 large artichoke
- 1 cup of water
- ¼ cup parmesan cheese (grated)
- ¼ tsp. salt
- ¼ tsp. red pepper flakes

Instructions

1. To prepare the artichoke, trim and remove the stem and outer leaves and top. Then spread the leaves purposefully
2. Pour the water to Instant Pot and place the steam rack on the pot's bottom. Place artichoke on the steam rack and sprinkle with parmesan, red pepper flakes, and salt. Firmly close the lid with the vent valve on "Sealing". Select the "Steam" option and set the time to 30 minutes.
3. Once the time is up, allow the natural pressure release for 15 minutes and then do a quick release of the remaining pressure.
4. Serve warm more parmesan.

Yield: 2 servings.

Nutritional content per serving: Calories: 135; Fat: 9 g; Net carbs: 4 g; Protein: 9 g.

Red Chili

Ingredients

- 4 slices bacon
- ½ lb. lean ground beef (preferably 85% lean)
- ½ lb. lean ground pork (preferably 84% lean)
- 1 green pepper (diced)
- ½ medium onion (diced)
- 2 cups beef broth
- 14.5 oz. tomatoes (diced; 1 can)
- 6 oz. tomato paste (1 can)
- 1 tbsp. chili powder
- 2 tsps. salt
- ½ tsp. pepper
- 1/8 tsp. cayenne
- ¼ tsp. xanthan gum (optional)

Instructions

1. Start the Instant Pot on the "Sauté" function and cook bacon. Then, remove, crumble, and set aside. Use the bacon grease to brown the beef and pork until fully cooked. Add onion and green pepper to the pot and cook for 1 minute to soften.
2. Press the "Cancel" button on the pot. With the exception of xanthan gum, combine the remaining ingredients in the pot. And tightly close the lid with the release valve set at Seal. Press the "Soup" button on the pot with the timer set for 30 minutes.
3. When the pot beeps to show the end of the cooking time, leave untouched for 10 minutes to naturally release the pressure. Then do a quick-release of the remaining pressure. Unlock the pot and stir in the bacon.
4. Serve warm and top with your chili toppings.
5. If you prefer a thicker chili, start the "Sauté" function as soon as you remove the lid after the quick release of the pressure. Reduce chill and increase xanthan gum. Keep stirring until desired thickness.
6. Add additional onions or other toppings.

Yield: 6 servings.

Nutritional content per serving: Calories: 219; Fat: 22.3 g; Net carbs: 2.4 g; Protein: 3.3g; Fiber: 0.8 g Sugar: 0.6 g.

Breakfast Burrito Bowl

Ingredients

- 6 eggs
- 3 tbsps. melted butter
- ¼ tsp. pepper
- 1 tsp. salt
- ½ lb. breakfast sausage (cooked)
- ½ cup sharp cheese (shredded)
- 1 avocado (cubed)
- ¼ cup green onion (diced)
- ½ cup salsa
- ½ cup sour cream

Instructions

1. Mix melted butter, eggs, pepper, and salt in a large bowl. Start the "Sauté" function on the Instant Pot and use the "Adjust" button to set it to cook on "Less".
2. Add the eggs mixture and cook for 5 - 7 minutes. Keep moving the rubber spatula gently until the eggs start thickening. Add the cheese and breakfast sausage and continue sautéing until fully cooked. Stop cooking by pressing the "Cancel" button.
3. Share eggs into serving bowls and top with avocado, green onion, salsa, and sour cream.

Yield: 4 servings.

Nutritional content per serving: Calories: 123; Fat: 39 g; Net carbs: 2 g;

Protein: 9 g.

Chocolate Cinnamon Roll Fat Bombs

Ingredients

- 2 tbsps. coconut oil
- 2 cups raw coconut butter
- 1 cup chocolate chips (sugar-free)
- 1 cup heavy whipping cream
- ½ cup swerve confectioners (or more, to taste)
- ½ tsp. ground cinnamon (or more, to taste)
- ½ tsp. vanilla extract

Instructions

1. Start the Instant Pot by pressing "Sauté" and add oil to melt.
2. Add the raw butter, chocolate chips, cream, cinnamon, confectioners, and vanilla extract to the Instant Pot and keep sautéing. Stir constantly to let the mixture reach a smooth consistency.
3. Then pour the mixture into a mini-muffin mold made of silicon.
4. Store in the freezer to let it until firm. (how long it will stay depends on the freezer temperature)
5. Serve when firm and enjoy!

Yield: 4 - 5 servings.

Nutritional content per serving: Calories: 372; Fat: 32.2 g; Net carbs: 15.1 g; Protein: 4.2 g; Fiber: 6.8 g Sugar: 0.1 g.

Creme Brulee

Ingredients

- 2 egg yolks
- 1 cup of filtered water
- 1 cup heavy whipping cream
- 1 tsp. vanilla extract
- ½ cup swerve confectioners (or more, to taste)
- 1/8 tsp. salt

Instructions

1. Pour the filtered water into the insert pot of the Instant Pot, and then insert the trivet. Combine egg yolks, cream, swerve, vanilla extract, and salt in a large bowl and mix thoroughly.
2. Share the mixture evenly into 5 well-greased Instant Pot-safe ramekins.
3. Carefully arrange the ramekins on the trivet one after the other. Loosely cover each small baking dish with aluminum foil.
4. Tightly close the lid and set the pressure release knob to "Sealing". Select "Manual/Pressure Cook" and adjust the Instant Pot timer to 7 minutes. Set to cook on "High Pressure".
5. Once the pot beeps to indicate the end of cook time, leave for about 10 minutes for the pressure to naturally disperse from the Instant Pot. Then switch the pressure release knob to "Venting" to disperse the remaining pressure. Thereafter, open and carefully remove the ramekins one after the other.
6. Allow to cool and then serve.

Yield: 5 servings.

Nutritional content per serving: Calories: 110; Fat: 10.2 g; Net carbs: 0.9 g; Protein: 2.7 g; Fiber: 0 g Sugar: 0.3 g.

Chocolate Chip Mini Muffins

Ingredients

- 1 cup of filtered water
- 1 cup almond flour (blanched)
- 2 eggs
- ¾ cup chocolate chips (sugar-free)
- 1 tbsp. vanilla extract
- ½ cup swerve confectioners (or more, to taste)
- 2 tbsps. butter (salted, grass-fed; softened)
- ½ tsp. salt
- ½ tsp. baking soda

Instructions

1. Pour the filtered water into the insert pot of the Instant Pot, and then insert the trivet. Use an electric mixer to combine eggs with, butter, chocolate chips, flour, swerve confectioners, salt, and baking soda. Mix well to combine. Transfer the mixture into a well-greased muffin or egg bites mold that is safe in the Instant Pot.
2. Carefully lower the mold onto the trivet in the pot, using a sling, if desired. Loosely cover with aluminum foil.
3. Tightly secure the lid, ensuring that the pressure release valve is set to "Sealing". Then press "Manual/Pressure Cook" and adjust the time to 20 minutes cooking on "High Pressure."
4. Once the pot beeps to signal the end of cooking, leave it for 10 minutes to release the pressure naturally. Then switch the pressure release valve to "Venting" to allow the remaining pressure to disperse.
5. Unlatch the lid and open the Instant Pot. Remove the pan and wait a few more minutes for the muffins to cool.
6. Serve and enjoy.

Yield: 7 servings.

Nutritional content per serving: Calories: 204; Fat: 17 g; Net carbs: 4 g; Protein: 3.1 g; Fiber: 1 g; Sugar: 7.4 g.

Sunrise Pizza

Ingredients (for crust)

- 2 eggs
- 2 tbsps. butter (salted, grass-fed; softened)
- 1 cup of filtered water
- 1 cup Parmesan cheese (full-fat; grated)
- 1 lb. chicken (ground)
- 1/3 cup almond flour (blanched)

Ingredients (for topping)

- 14 oz. fire-roasted tomatoes (sugar-free or low-sugar; less than 1 can; drained)
- 2 cups mozzarella cheese (full-fat, shredded)
- 1 cup spinach (chopped)
- ½ tsp. basil (dried)
- ½ tsp. cilantro (dried)
- ½ tsp. oregano (dried)
- ½ tsp. red pepper (crushed)

Instructions

1. Pour the filtered water into the insert pot of the Instant Pot, and then insert the trivet. Combine the eggs with butter, cheese, ground chicken, and flour in a large mixing bowl and mix thoroughly. Transfer the mixture into a well-greased dish that is Instant Pot-safe.

2. Carefully lower the dish onto the trivet in the pot, using a sling, if desired. Loosely cover with aluminum foil.

3. Tightly secure the lid, ensuring that the pressure release valve is set to "Sealing". Then press "Manual/Pressure Cook" and adjust the time to 10 minutes cooking on "High Pressure" and start cooking.

4. Meanwhile, mix basil, cilantro, oregano, and red pepper in a small bowl. Set aside as parts of topping.

5. Once cooked, carefully switch the pressure release valve to "Venting" to allow the pressure to disperse. Open the Instant Pot when it is safe to do so and evenly add the tomatoes in a layer, and then the cheese and the spinach. Sprinkle the top of the pizza with the spice and herb mixture. Cover the dish back loosely with the same aluminum foil.

6. Repeat the cooking, but now the time should be set to 10 minutes on high pressure.

7. Once the pot beeps to signal the end of cooking, leave it for 10 minutes to release the pressure naturally. Then switch the pressure release valve to "Venting" to allow the remaining pressure to disperse.

8. Open the pot, serve the pizza warm, and enjoy!

Yield: 5 servings.

Nutritional content per serving: Calories: 405; Fat: 21 g; Net carbs: 2.5 g; Protein: 21.9 g; Fiber: 0.9 g; Sugar: 1.5 g

Cheddar-Herbed Strata

Ingredients

- 6 eggs
- 1 cup of filtered water
- 1 cup Cheddar cheese (full-fat; shredded)
- 1 cup spinach (chopped)
- ½ tbsp. butter (salted, grass-fed; softened)
- 4 oz. onion (¼ small onion; thinly sliced)
- ½ tsp. black pepper (freshly ground)
- ½ tsp. kosher salt
- ½ tsp. Dijon mustard
- ½ tsp. paprika
- ½ tsp. cayenne pepper
- ½ tsp. cilantro dried
- ½ tsp. sage (dried)
- ½ tsp. parsley (dried)

Instructions

1. Pour the filtered water into the insert pot of the Instant Pot, and then insert the trivet. Combine eggs with, butter, black pepper, cayenne pepper, cheese, cilantro, mustard, parsley, paprika, sage, spinach, onion, salt, and baking soda. Mix well to combine. Transfer the mixture into a well-greased dish that is safe in the Instant Pot.
2. Carefully lower the dish onto the trivet in the pot, using a sling, if desired. Loosely cover with aluminum foil.
3. Tightly secure the lid, ensuring that the pressure release valve is set to "Sealing". Then press "Manual/Pressure Cook" and adjust the time to 40 minutes cooking on "High Pressure." Start cooking.
4. Once the pot beeps to signal the end of cooking, leave it for 10 minutes to release the pressure naturally. Then switch the pressure release valve to "Venting" to allow the remaining pressure to disperse.
5. Unlatch the lid and open the Instant Pot. Remove the dish and wait a few minutes to cool
6. Serve and enjoy.

Yield: 4 servings.

Nutritional content per serving: Calories: 179; Fat: 7.2 g; Net carbs: 2 g; Protein: 10.3 g; Fiber: 0.6 g; Sugar: 0.8 g.

Traditional Coffee Cake

Ingredients (for base)
- 2 eggs
- 1 cup of filtered water
- 2 tbsps. butter (salted grass-fed; softened)
- 1 cup almond flour (blanched)
- 1 cup pecans (chopped)
- ¼ cup sour cream (at room temperature)
- ¼ cup cream cheese (full-fat; softened)
- ½ tsp. salt
- ½ tsp. cinnamon (ground)
- ½ tsp. nutmeg (ground)
- ¼ tsp. baking soda

Ingredients (for topping)
- 1 cup chocolate chips (sugar-free)
- 1 cup pecans (chopped)
- ½ cup swerve confectioners (or more, to taste)
- ½ cup heavy whipping cream

Instructions
1. Pour the filtered water into the insert pot of the Instant Pot, and then insert the trivet. Use an electric mixer to combine the eggs with butter, cream cheese, cinnamon, nutmeg, flour, pecans, sour cream, salt, and baking soda. Mix well to form. Transfer the mixture into a well-greased pan that is safe in the Instant Pot.
2. Carefully lower the pan onto the trivet in the pot, using a sling, if desired. Loosely cover with aluminum foil.
3. Tightly secure the lid, ensuring that the pressure release valve is set to "Sealing". Then press "Manual/Pressure Cook" and adjust the time to 40 minutes cooking on "High Pressure." Start cooking.
4. Meanwhile, mix thoroughly chocolate chips, confectionary, pecan, and whipping cream in a large bowl. Set aside.
5. Once the pot beeps to signal the end of cooking, leave for 10 minutes to allow the natural release of pressure. Then move the pressure release knob to "Venting" to do a quick release of the remaining pressure.
6. Unlatch the lid to open and remove the pan. Sprinkle the topping mixture evenly over the cake. Wait to let cool and then serve.

Yield: 5 - 6 servings.

Nutritional content per serving: Calories: 267; Fat: 22.7 g; Net carbs: 4.4 g; Protein: 7.3 g; Fiber: 1.6 g; Sugar: 0.8 g.

Coconut Milk Berry Smoothie

Ingredients

- 2 tbsps. butter (grass-fed; softened)
- 1 ¼ of filtered water
- 2/3 cup coconut milk (full fat)
- 10 drops liquid stevia
- 2 tbsps. unflavored MCT oil
- 2 tbsps. flax seeds (soaked)
- 2 tbsps. chocolate chips (sugar-free; optional)
- ½ tsp. turmeric (ground)
- ½ tsp. nutmeg (ground)
- ¼ cup heavy whipping cream
- ¼ cup mixed dark berries (it could be blueberries/strawberries or blackberries/raspberries)
- 2 scoops protein powder (grass-fed whey)
- Ice cubes to serve

Instructions

1. Pour the filtered water into a standing blender (the quantity to be used will depend on the individual taste of thickness of sweetness).
2. Start the Instant Pot on "Sauté" and add the butter to melt.
3. Add coconut milk, chocolate chips, flax seeds, MCT oil, nutmeg, stevia, turmeric, whipping cream, and dark berries, stirring continuously.
4. Stop sauté program by hitting "Cancel" on the pot once everything is mixed thoroughly. Remove the insert of the Instant Pot, and carefully pour the content in a blender.
5. Add the protein powder to the mixture and blend to your desired consistency.
6. Fill tall glasses with ice cubes and serve the smoothie mixture in it. The leftovers can be stored in an airtight container for up to 30 in the freezer and up to 2 days in the refrigerator.

Yield: 3 servings.

Nutritional content per serving: Calories: 431; Fat: 39.7 g; Net carbs: 6.6 g; Protein: 14.6 g; Fiber: 4.4 g; Sugar: 3.4 g.

CHAPTER 21: DESSERTS AND CAKES RECIPES

Desserts are as important as the main course. What you eat last gives a lasting impression about the meal. That is why you love to have foods like cakes and smoothies as the last thing. The Instant Pot with its pressure cooking technology can add some enhancements to your breakfast, lunch, or dinner desserts. Consider a few recipes for such Instant Pot-compatible desserts.

Pumpkin Pie Custard

Ingredients

- 2 cups fresh pumpkin puree (or 2 cans pure pumpkin 15-ounce
- 6 eggs
- 1 cup full fat coconut milk
- ¾ cup pure maple syrup (or light-colored raw honey)
- 1 tbsp. Pumpkin Pie Spice
- ¾ tsp. lemon zest (finely grated)
- 2 tsp. pure vanilla extract
- ¼ tsp. sea salt
- 2 cups of lukewarm water

Instructions

1. Whisk the pumpkin puree and eggs together with the coconut milk, lemon zest, maple syrup, pumpkin pie spice, vanilla extract, and salt. Fill the 6 ramekins evenly with the mixture.
2. Pour the water into the Instant Pot with the wire rack placed at the bottom.
3. Cover the ramekins with silicone lids or foil and arrange them carefully on the wire rack.
4. Adjust the setting of your Instant pot to "Manual or Pressure Cook". Set the timer for 6 minutes and the pressure on "High".
5. After the 6 minutes cook time, leave the pot for about 20 to 25 minutes to naturally release the pressure. When the pressure has returned to normal, take the ramekins out of the pot. Remove the foil or silicon lids and leave it to cool completely on the wire rack.
6. Safe the ramekins in plastic wrap and place in the refrigerator for not more than 5 days.

Yield: 6 servings.

Apple Pie Applesauce

Ingredients

- 3 ½ lbs. assorted sweet and tart apples (such as Fuji, Gala, or Granny Smith; to be peeled, cored, and sliced)
- 2 tsps. lemon juice (freshly squeezed)
- ¾ cup of water
- 2 tsps. ghee
- ¼ tsp ground cinnamon (add more for serving)
- 1/8 tsp. ground allspice
- 1/8 tsp. fine sea salt

Instructions

1. Add the water, allspice, cinnamon, ghee, lemon juice, and salt in an Instant Pot. Mix well and add the apple.
2. Tightly secure the lid and turn the pressure release valve to "Sealing". Adjust the setting of your Instant pot to "Manual or Pressure Cook". Set the timer for 15 minutes and the pressure on "High". Once the pot beeps to signal the end of cook time, leave the pot for about 20 minutes to naturally release the pressure and/or do a quick release of pressure. When the pressure has returned to normal, unlock the lid and open the pot.
3. Insert an immersion blender and puree the applesauce to the desired consistency. If you don't have an immersion blender, you may pour it into a standing blender.
4. Then serve warm, sprinkling cinnamon on top. You may allow it to cool and refrigerate for a few hours. Then serve chilled.
5. If stored, in an airtight container, it can be refrigerated for up to 10 days or stored in a freezer for up to 6 months. If stored in a freezer, transfer it to the refrigerator to thaw overnight before serving.
6. You may also reheat for 8 to 10 minutes in by pressing "Sauce" in the Instant Pot.

Yield: 6 servings.

Vanilla-Scented Rice Pudding

Ingredients (dry ingredients)

- ¼ tsp. sea salt
- ¼ tsp. cinnamon
- ¼ cup brown sugar
- 1 whole vanilla bean (split along one side)
- 3 cups arborio (or short-grain white rice)
- ¾ cup raisins

Ingredients (for cooking and serving)

- 4 ½ cups of water
- ½ cup heavy cream (or coconut cream)

Instructions

1. To prepare, arrange all dry ingredients in a jar the listed order.
2. Pour the content of the jar into the Instant Pot and add the water. Mix everything.
3. Tightly secure the lid and turn the pressure release valve to "Sealing". Adjust the setting of your Instant pot to "Manual or Pressure Cook". Set the timer for 8 minutes and the pressure on "High". At the end of cook time, leave the pot for about 10 minutes for the naturally release the pressure. Then do a quick release of remaining pressure.
4. Unlock the lid, open the pot, and stir in any cream used. Let it wait for no more than 5 minutes and serve.

Yield: 6 - 8 servings.

Mixed Berry Mousse

Ingredients

- 20 oz. thawed frozen blackberries (about 4 cups; can be chosen from blueberries, raspberries, and strawberries)
- 6 tbsps. sugar (divided)
- 1 tsp. lemon zest (finely grated)
- Pinch table salt
- 1 ½ tsp. gelatin (unflavored)
- ½ cup heavy cream
- 3 oz. cream cheese (softened)

Instructions

1. Combine berries, lemon zest, 3 tablespoons of sugar, and salt in a bowl. Set aside for about 30 minutes while stirring occasionally.
2. Use a fine mesh strainer to strain the berries over a separate bowl. Transfer the strained berries to the Ace blender and set aside. Pour 3 tablespoons of drained juice into a small bowl. Sprinkle with gelatin and allow to wait until gelatin softens, not more than 6 minutes.
3. Meanwhile, set the remaining juice in a microwave for 4 to 5 minutes until reduced to 3 tablespoons or so. Whisk gelatin mixture and remaining 3 tablespoons sugar into reduced juice until dissolved.
4. Lock blender lid and process berries on "Medium" speed for about 30 seconds or until smooth. Then add gelatin mixture, cream cheese, and heavy cream, and process again for about 10 seconds on "Medium" speed or until well combined. Then process again on "High" for about 30 seconds or until smooth. Pause occasionally to scrape down the sides of the blender jar.
5. Divide the mousse into 4 serving dishes and refrigerate in a covered plastic for at least 4 hours until set, but not more than 48 hours.
6. Serve.

Yield: 4 - 6 servings.

Mini Mochaccino Cheesecakes

Ingredients (for crust)

- Cooking spray (or oil)
- ½ cup old-fashioned oats
- 8 almonds (whole, raw)
- ¼ cup cocoa (unsweetened)
- 2 tbsps. granulated sugar
- 3 tbsps. unsalted butter (melted)
- 1/8 tsp. salt

Ingredients (cheesecake filling)

- 6 oz. cream cheese (cubed and room temperature)
- 1 tbsp. sour cream (at room temperature)
- 1 cup of water
- ¼ tsp. vanilla extract
- 2 tsps. instant espresso powder
- ¼ cup granulated sugar
- 1 large egg (at room temperature)

Instructions

1. To prepare the crust, rub six silicone cupcake liners lightly with either the cooking spray or oil.
2. Pulse oats, almonds, butter, cocoa, sugar, and salt in a small food processor. Pour the crumb mixture into liners. Press down each along the bottom and 1/3 of the way up the sides.
3. To prepare the cheesecake filling, use an immersion blender or food processor to cream together the cheese, espresso powder, vanilla, and sugar. Pulse to smoothness and gradually add the egg. Then pulse for another 10 seconds. Keep scraping the bowl as you continue to pulse until the batter is smooth. Transfer batter into cupcake liners.
4. Pour the water into the Instant Pot and Insert the steam rack. Lower the steamer basket on the steam rack. Then carefully arrange cheesecakes in the steamer basket.
5. Tightly lock the lid. Adjust the setting of your Instant pot to "Manual or Pressure Cook". Set the timer for 20 minutes. At the end of cook time, do a quick release of the pressure.
6. Take the steamer basket out of the pot and expose the cheese for 10 minutes to cool to the room temperature.
7. To let the somewhat jiggly firm and set, store in the fridge for at least 1 hour.

Yield: 6 servings.

Fudgy Chocolate Cake

Ingredients

- ½ cup butter
- 1 cup sugar
- 1 tsp. vanilla
- 2 large eggs
- ¾ cup flour
- ½ cup cocoa powder
- 1 tsp. baking powder
- ½ tsp. salt
- 1 cup chocolate chips
- 1 cup of water

Instructions

1. Using an electric mixer, cream the butter, sugar, and vanilla until fluffy and light in a large bowl. At one time, beat in eggs until well-combined.
2. Whisk together the cocoa, flour, baking powder, and salt in a small bowl. Gradually add both mixtures of flour and eggs and keep stirring as you are adding until well-combined. Stir in the chocolate.
3. Spoon batter into an 8-inch nonstick springform pan. Smooth the top and cover with aluminum foil. Pour the water into the Instant Pot and lower the wire trivet to the pot bottom while the pan is set on top.
4. Tightly lock the lid on the pot and set the vent valve into "Sealing". Set cook on "Pressure Cook or Manual" on "High Pressure" for 30 minutes.
5. After the cook time, allow 10-minute natural pressure release and quick-release the remaining pressure.
6. Cut into wedges while still warm, and serve.

Yield: 4 - 6 servings.

Family Size Buttermilk Pancake

Ingredients

- 1 ½ cups flour
- 1 tsp. baking powder
- ¼ tsp. salt
- 2 tbsps. butter (melted)
- 1 cup buttermilk
- 2 large eggs
- 1 cup of water
- 3 tbsps. sugar
- 2 tbsps. vegetable shortening (or butter)
- Favorite pancake toppings

Instructions

1. Whisk together the baking powder, flour, and salt in a mixing bowl. In another bowl, whisk together the butter, buttermilk, eggs, water, and sugar. Stir the mixture into the dry ingredients all is well-combined.
2. Spread the vegetable shortening or butter in the bottom and up the sides (2 inches) of the Instant Pot. Then pour in the batter.
3. Lock the lid into place ensuring that the vent valve is on "Sealing". Cook on "Low Pressure" with the timer set for 40 minutes. (Some pots have "Cake" setting, use that if yours has instead of "Low Pressure".) When the cooking stops and the timer beeps, leave for 10-minute the natural pressure release. Then use the quick pressure release.
4. Run a rubber spatula around the edge of the pancake to remove to smoothly and transfer onto a plate. Then cut into wedges and serve. Add any topping of your choice.

Yield: 4 - 6 servings.

Traditional Cupcakes

Ingredients (for cake)

- 2 cups almond flour (blanched)
- 1 cup of filtered water
- ½ tsp. baking powder
- 2 tbsps. butter (grass-fed, softened)
- ½ cup almond milk (unsweetened)
- 2 eggs
- ½ cup Swerve confectioners (or more, to taste)
- ½ tsp. nutmeg (ground)

Ingredients (for frosting)

- 4 oz. cream cheese (full-fat, softened)
- 4 tbsps. grass-fed butter (softened)
- 2 cups heavy whipping cream
- 1 tsp. vanilla extract
- ½ cup Swerve confectioners (or more, to taste)
- 6 tbsps. chocolate chips (sugar-free, optional

Instructions

1. Pour filtered water into the insert of the Instant Pot and insert the trivet. In a large bowl, combine the all ingredients of cake apart from the water together and mix thoroughly. Spoon the mixture into well-greased muffin molds or egg bites molds. Do this in batches.
2. Place the molds with their contents onto the trivet. Cover loosely with aluminum foil.
3. Tightly close the lid with the pressure release set to "Sealing." Select "Manual or Pressure Cook" and adjust the timer to 30 minutes. Cook on "High" Pressure.
4. In the meantime, combine all the ingredients for frosting in a large bowl. Using an electric hand mixer, mix thoroughly until you have a fluffy and light texture. Keep the frosting in the refrigerator.
5. When the timer beeps notifying you that the cupcakes are cooked, allow the pressure to release naturally for about 10 minutes and then, turn the pressure release valve to "Venting" to release the remaining pressure.
6. Open the pot and remove the pan. Allow it cool and evenly top each cupcake with frosting.
7. Serve and enjoy it after a nice meal.

Yield: 7 servings.

CONCLUSION

Who has all the time in this complex modern world to keep a watchful eye on what is cooking? Folks are fed up of staying up to have that delicious meal. Little wonder junks are being crunched all around in the name of tastiness and time factor. You need to take advantage of technology to cook healthy food delightfully. Gone are those days when you have to find it tasking to prepare food and spend all the hours doing so.

The cookbook has highlighted 200+ recipes that can add more values to your cooking in the Instant Pot. The 10 -13 recipes in each of the 19 categories are by no means all there is to those recipes. However, trying and tasting them will give you a sample of the yums waiting for you to enjoy. You would then see how your palate and stomach will react to your body and mood when you treat them to nice meals you find their recipes here.

Take your time to try them all. You may not have to rush through them. But one thing I can assure you is this: There is none of them that you try that will not boost your appreciation for this book. You will certainly want to recommend what you read here for friends and folks.

Take it from here, you can cook all you want to cook in the Instant Pot and enjoy your cooking and your food!

Made in the
USA
Monee, IL